It is now well-established that spelling can facilitate or interfere with pronunciation learning in an additional language. This book provides an indispensable analysis of the enormous influence that orthography can have on pronunciation learning. Its extensive research on orthographic effects demonstrates how orthography impacts target language production, perception, and awareness, as well as the potential success of teaching interventions.

—***John Levis**, Iowa State University, USA*

Effects of Orthography on Second Language Phonology

This is the first book devoted to the effects of orthographic forms (spellings) on second language phonology.

Written by one of the pioneer researchers in the field, the book provides an authoritative overview of the effects of spelling on the perception, production, awareness, learning, and teaching of sounds and spoken words in a second language. Using the findings and implications from a large-scale research project at its centre, the book reveals that English consonants spelled with double letters lead Italian learners and users of English as a second language to perceive, produce, classify, and learn English consonants as geminates (long consonants).

Presenting a narrative of a second language research project and discussing its implications, the book will be of interest to scholars and researchers in the fields of orthography, phonology, speech, and language perception. Language teaching practitioners will also find the book useful.

Bene Bassetti is Associate Professor of Applied Linguistics at the University of Modena and Reggio Emilia, Italy, and Senior Honorary Research Fellow at the University of Birmingham, United Kingdom.

Routledge Research in Language Education

The *Routledge Research in Language Education* series provides a platform for established and emerging scholars to present their latest research and discuss key issues in Language Education. This series welcomes books on all areas of language teaching and learning, including but not limited to language education policy and politics, multilingualism, literacy, L1, L2 or foreign language acquisition, curriculum, classroom practice, pedagogy, teaching materials, and language teacher education and development. Books in the series are not limited to the discussion of the teaching and learning of English only.

Books in the series include:

Typical and Atypical Language Development in Cultural and Linguistic Diversity
Edited by Weifeng Han and Chris Brebner

Assessment of Plurilingual Competence and Plurilingual Learners in Educational Settings
Educative Issues and Empirical Approaches
Edited by Sílvia Melo-Pfeifer and Christian Ollivier

Early Childhood Language Education and Literacy Practices in Ethiopia
Perspectives from Indigenous Knowledge, Gender, and Instructional Practices
Edited by Kassahun Weldemariam, Margareth Sandvik and Moges Yigezu

Effects of Orthography on Second Language Phonology
Learning, Awareness, Perception and Production
Bene Bassetti

For more information about the series, please visit www.routledge.com/Routledge-Research-in-Language-Education/book-series/RRLE

Effects of Orthography on Second Language Phonology
Learning, Awareness, Perception, and Production

Bene Bassetti

LONDON AND NEW YORK

First published 2023
by Routledge
4 Park Square, Milton Park, Abingdon, Oxon OX14 4RN

and by Routledge
605 Third Avenue, New York, NY 10158

Routledge is an imprint of the Taylor & Francis Group, an informa business

© 2023 Bene Bassetti

The right of Bene Bassetti to be identified as author of this work has been asserted in accordance with sections 77 and 78 of the Copyright, Designs and Patents Act 1988.

All rights reserved. No part of this book may be reprinted or reproduced or utilised in any form or by any electronic, mechanical, or other means, now known or hereafter invented, including photocopying and recording, or in any information storage or retrieval system, without permission in writing from the publishers.

Trademark notice: Product or corporate names may be trademarks or registered trademarks, and are used only for identification and explanation without intent to infringe.

British Library Cataloguing-in-Publication Data
A catalogue record for this book is available from the British Library

ISBN: 978-0-367-34847-2 (hbk)
ISBN: 978-1-032-59610-5 (pbk)
ISBN: 978-0-429-34311-7 (ebk)

DOI: 10.4324/9780429343117

Typeset in Times New Roman
by Apex CoVantage, LLC

I dedicate my first monograph to Professor Vivian Cook (1940–2021), who for over twenty years affectionately showed me how to be an applied linguist.

Contents

	Acknowledgements	*x*
1	Background: Key concepts in L+ phonology and orthography	1
2	Effects of orthography on L+ phonology: An overview	10
3	Effects of orthography on L+ phonology: A case study	28
4	Effects of orthography on L+ speech production	46
5	Effects of orthography on L+ awareness, perception, and learning	63
6	Characteristics, causes, and implications of orthographic effects on L+ phonology	88
	Index	*110*

Acknowledgements

My deep gratitude goes to my co-investigator, Professor Jackie Masterson, for always coming to the rescue in moments of crisis, mentoring, and supporting me throughout. I am very grateful to the postdoctoral researchers who contributed so much to this project: Dr Tania Cerni, who raised the level of sophistication in statistical analyses; Dr Paolo Mairano, who was responsible for anything related to phonetics and phonology; Dr Mirjana Sokolovic-Perovic, who took over much of my teaching and contributed a brilliant idea; and Dr Alex Panicacci, who single-handedly recruited and tested all UK participants. Thanks also go to the advisory board members who helped improve the quality of the project, David Torgerson and Richard Ogden, and to the research assistants who contributed to acoustic analyses: Drs Nathan Atkinson, Emanuela Buizza, Valentina De Iacovo, and Alessandra Nodari. I owe an immense debt to the English language teachers who agreed to support this project for what probably felt like a very long school year and to all participants, particularly the high-school students who underwent testing for hours for the sake of science. Finally, I am very grateful to the Leverhulme Trust for believing in the project and supporting it.

1 Background
Key concepts in L+ phonology and orthography

Background

This is the first book devoted to the effects of orthographic forms (spellings) on second language phonology — the perception, production, awareness, learning, and spelling of sounds and spoken words in a non-native language. The first part reviews this burgeoning area of research, and the second part reports the methods, findings, and implications of a research project that investigated the effects of an aspect of English spelling (number of letters) on all second language phonology processes (perception, production, awareness, and learning) in speakers of English as a second language.

This first chapter briefly introduces the basic concepts, terms, and conventions that are used in the book. These are illustrated with examples from standard British English, which is the language investigated by the research project described here. Readers who are familiar with these topics can skip, or skim through, the chapter.

Introduction to L+ phonology

Second language phonology — called 'L+ phonology' in this book — aims at describing and explaining the learning, representation, and processing of the speech sounds of a language learned after the native one(s).

Defining L+ phonology

The L+. A language that is learnt after acquiring the first (or native) language(s) (L1) is usually called a 'second language' (L2). This book instead uses the term 'plus language', or 'L+'. While 'second' may have negative connotations ('next in order of importance') and is not suitable for a chronologically third or later language (Dewaele, 2017), 'plus' has positive connotations and can indicate any language beyond the first one(s) ('additional' is used in the United Kingdom for the English of children with home languages other than English).

DOI: 10.4324/9780429343117-1

2 Key concepts in L+ phonology and orthography

This book then talks about *L+ learners* (those who are in the process of learning an L+, formally or informally, after acquiring their first language or languages) and *L+ users*, or *sequential bilinguals* (those who know and use a language they learnt after acquiring their L1(s), that is to say, former L+ learners).

Phonology. The term 'phonology' in 'L+ phonology' covers both the actual sounds of languages and the abstract sound systems of languages (Levis & Munro, 2012). In linguistics, these are two separate branches. Phonetics investigates the physical properties of speech (such as sound duration), speech perception, and speech production (how the phonatory system, including the lips and vocal cords, produces speech). Phonology investigates the categories and patterns of sound systems. L+ phonology researchers instead pragmatically adopt the theories and methods from both phonetics and phonology that are most useful when investigating L+ phonology.

The object of L+ phonology research

Speech sounds and features. Phonology investigates the sounds of language. Each language has a phonological inventory, which is a set of speech sounds — also called *phonemes* — that can distinguish two words in that language (Ladefoged & Maddieson, 1996). In the English language, we know that [b] and [p] are different phonemes because they distinguish, for instance, *cab* and *cap*. The lexical contrast *cab-cap* is evidence of the phonological contrast [b]-[p]. Two words that only differ in one sound, such as *cab-cap*, are called a *minimal pair*.

Characteristics of a sound production that can distinguish phonemes are called *distinctive features*. For instance, [b] and [p] are produced with the same mouth shape, and the difference is that [b] is voiced (the vocal folds vibrate) and [p] is voiceless (the vocal folds do not vibrate). Therefore, [voice] is a distinctive feature.

Sounds that are different realisations of the same phoneme are called *allophones*. For instance, in English, the phoneme [p] is aspirated (produced with a puff of air) in word-initial position (*pig*) and unaspirated in other positions (*sip*). These are allophones because there are no minimal pairs contrasting aspirated and unaspirated [p], and the feature of aspiration is not distinctive.

Consonants and vowels. Speech sounds, or *segments*, are divided into consonants and vowels. Vowels involve no stricture (narrowing of the vocal tract that affects the airstream) and may constitute a syllable by themselves. Consonants involve some stricture and need to be pronounced with (before or after) a vowel (Ladefoged & Maddieson, 1996).

Consonants are described using three articulatory features — for instance, [t] is a 'voiceless alveolar stop' — as follows:

1 Voicing: Whether vocal cords vibrate. For instance, [t] is voiceless and [d] is voiced

Key concepts in L+ phonology and orthography 3

2 Place of articulation: Parts of the phonatory system involved in the stricture. For instance, bilabials involve both lips ([b]); labiodentals involve lips and teeth ([f])
3 Manner of articulation: The position of the articulators (parts of the vocal tract that produce speech sounds, such as the tongue and lips). If the articulators stop air completely and then release it, it is a plosive ([t]); if the oral cavity is closed and air exits through the nose, it is a nasal ([n]).

Vowels are described in terms of height (how much the tongue is raised: High/mid/low), backness (which part of the tongue is most raised: Front/centre/back), and lip rounding (rounded/unrounded). For instance, the vowel in *hit* is a high front unrounded vowel.

Other areas of investigation. Phonology also studies *phonotactics*, which determines which sound sequences are permitted in a language, for instance, whether it allows consonant clusters and, if so, which consonant sequences are allowed. It also studies suprasegmentals, or prosody, which are phenomena above the level of consonants and vowels, such as stress (which marks the most prominent, longer, louder sound).

Symbols and conventions

Speech is transcribed using the International Phonetic Alphabet (IPA). Slashes (/ta/) and square brackets ([ta]) delimit a phonological form (slashes are used in phonology and square brackets in phonetics, but the distinction is not always straightforward). Angle brackets (<ta>) indicate an orthographic form, italics indicate a piece of language (regardless of whether written or spoken), and quotation marks indicate a translation. For instance, the Italian word *nota* ('note') is pronounced [ˈnɔta] and spelled <nota>.

This book uses IPA symbols for consonants and vowels, plus the following:

- /ˈ/ Primary stress: Marks the following syllable as the most stressed in the word (/ˌkɒnsəˈnæntl/, *consonantal*)
- /ˌ/ Secondary stress: Marks the following syllable as the second most stressed in the word (ˌkɒnsəˈnæntl/)
- /ː/ Length mark: Marks the preceding sound as long (/ʃiːp/, *sheep*)
- /./ Syllable break.

Main issues in L+ phonology research

This section reviews the main findings and theories of L+ phonology research that are relevant to the project presented in this volume. Compared with monolingual native speakers of their target language, L+ speakers have different mental representations of the phonological categories of their L+, and perceive and produce L+ sounds differently. This is because L+ speakers start learning L+ phonology after having acquired the phonology of their L1(s), and indeed, the characteristics of the L1 phonology affect the acquisition and processing of an L+ phonology, although other variables also play a role.

Effects of first language phonology

The phonology of the native language(s) strongly influences L+ phonology, as L+ learners need to perceive and articulate sounds that differ from similar L1 sounds, as well as learning sounds that do not exist in the L1. L+ listeners often assimilate an L+ sound into an L1 sound. The effects of the L1 on the L+ (or indeed any effects of knowing a language on another language) are called *cross-linguistic influence* or *transfer*. Effects are found in L+ speech perception, speech production, and phonological awareness at the levels of global accent and specific sounds.

- *Speech perception.* L1 phonological categories often influence the perception of L+ sounds. For instance, an Italian$_{L1}$ listener may perceive English$_{L+}$ [ð] (*this*) as [d], because [ð] does not exist in Italian and the closest L1 sound is [d]. They may also perceive English$_{L+}$ [ɪ] as the similarly sounding Italian$_{L1}$ [i]. Indeed, L+ contrast discrimination is difficult when the L+ has two contrasting sounds that do not contrast in the learner's L1, as in Italians' perception of the English$_{L+}$ lax-tense [ɪ] and [iː] vowel contrast (Italian has no such phonemic contrast)
- A crucial concept in speech perception is *categorical perception*. Native listeners perceive distinct categories in a continuum; for instance, if they are asked to listen to different sounds in-between [p] and [b], English natives categorise some sounds along this continuum as /p/ and others as /b/, with a clear boundary between the two. L+ listeners whose L1 does not distinguish /p-b/ may label both sounds as one category or may distinguish two categories but with fuzzy boundaries
- *Speech production.* Some difficulties in L+ production may be caused by difficulties in perception, as learners must arguably be able to recognise sounds before they can produce them. There may also be difficulties related to the actual articulation of L+ sounds. Hence, Italians may replace [ð] with [d] because they perceive [ð] as [d], or because they cannot articulate the sound [ð] correctly, or for both reasons
- *Phonological awareness.* Phonological awareness is the conscious knowledge of the units of sound of language — such as phonemes and syllables — and is shown by the ability to identify and manipulate them, for instance, by counting the sounds in a word (for instance, *tool* contains three sounds). The L1 can affect, for instance, how many sounds one counts in an L+ word (Vaid et al., 2022).

However, simply contrasting the phonologies of the two languages cannot predict the outcomes of L+ phonology acquisition. There are aspects of phonological acquisition that are universal, being found in the acquisition of all languages, and in L1 as well as L+ phonology acquisition. These include, for example, deleting consonants from consonant clusters and substituting word-final voiced obstruent consonants with voiceless ones (which are easier to articulate).

Other variables that affect L+ phonology

A number of variables other than L1 phonology also affect L+ phonology.

Age of onset of acquisition (AOA) is the age at which the learner started being exposed to the L+. Although L+ phonological acquisition is possible at any age (Piske et al., 2001), those first exposed after childhood are likely to have a foreign accent (Abrahamsson & Hyltenstam, 2009).

Other individual and environmental variables. Apart from age and L1, other variables appear to have an impact, including *phonological aptitude*, the ability to discriminate, memorise, recall, and mimic unfamiliar sounds (see Piske et al., 2001); *phonological short-term memory*, the ability to retain sounds in memory while processing them (Darcy et al., 2015); *integrative motivation* (Shively, 2008); and the importance of native-like pronunciation to the L+ speaker (Suter, 1976). Other variables appear to have inconsistent effects across studies, including length of residence in an L+ environment (Derwing & Munro, 2015) and L+ proficiency (Iwashita et al., 2008). Other variables appear to have no effect, including length of instruction (Flege & Fletcher, 1992).

Finally, it should be noted that the teaching or training of target sounds often has positive effects, although some studies found no effect, and its efficacy depends on variables such as the difficulty of the L+ sound (for reviews, see Lee et al., 2015; Saito & Plonsky, 2019).

Models of L+ phonology development

Scholars have proposed different models to explain the development of L+ phonology. The two presented here inspired much empirical research.

- The *Perceptual Assimilation Model* (*PAM-L2*, Best & Tyler, 2007) aims at explaining the acquisition of L+ phonological contrasts, particularly in the early stages. The level of difficulty in perceiving the two contrasting L+ sounds depends on the number of similar phonological categories in L1. When one L1 sound corresponds to two contrasting L+ sounds, the two L+ sounds are categorised as one sound. For instance, Japanese listeners perceive English$_{L+}$ /l/ and /r/ as the same consonant because Japanese$_{L1}$ has only one liquid. Discrimination is easier if the L1 and L+ have a similar

phonological contrast, for instance, English$_{L+}$ /θ-ð/ can be perceived as a contrast, similarly to L1 /t-d/
- The revised *Speech Learning Model (SLM-r*, Flege & Bohn, 2021; see also Flege, 1995), aims at explaining the lifelong development of L+ sounds in a naturalistic environment. To perceive and produce the L+, the learner needs to create new categories based on phonetic input. This is easier if an L+ sound is identical to, or totally different from, an L1 sound. If an L+ sound is phonetically close to an L1 sound, the learner develops a composite L1-L2 category.

Another relevant model is Escudero's *Second Language Linguistic Perception Model* (*L2LP* revised in Van Leussen & Escudero, 2015) which models the development of L+ perception over time. Similarly to PAM-L2, this model predicts most difficulty when the L+ has more categories than the L1 (the 'new' scenario), similar to the 'single category assimilation' in PAM-L2.

Finally, in the field, there is a debate on the relationship between L+ perception and production, which is relevant to the study reported later. While some researchers believe that perception must precede production, others believe that perception and production develop independently of each other (for a discussion, see Colantoni et al., 2015).

The goals of L+ phonology learning

Before concluding this brief excursus, in order to discuss orthographic effects (OEs) on L+ phonology, it is important to clarify what the goal of L+ phonology acquisition is. While comparisons between L1 and L+ speakers are generally inappropriate, they can be useful in research on the effects of orthography.

Traditionally, the target of L+ phonology acquisition was native-likeness, and L+ speakers' performance was measured against monolingual native speakers. This comparison is inappropriate because someone who learned another language after the first one cannot, by definition, be either a monolingual or a native speaker of the later-learnt language. They 'should be considered in their own right, not as a monolingual who has tacked another language on to their repertoire' (Cook, 2016, p. 252).

Current research on L+ speech production (since Munro & Derwing, 1995) avoids native-likeness and focusses on:

1 *Intelligibility* — whether a listener can understand the L+ speaker, for instance, whether the L+ speaker said *clown* or *crown*
2 *Comprehensibility* — how difficult it is to understand the L+ speaker, for instance, how long it takes or whether repetitions are required to understand whether they said *clown* or *crown*
3 *Accentedness* — how different the L+ speaker's production is from the target, for instance, how much they obstruct the airflow when producing [l] in *clown*.

Key concepts in L+ phonology and orthography 7

These are also measures of L+ speech perception. For instance, can the L+ listener understand whether the word they heard was *clown* or *crown* (intelligibility); how difficult it is for them to understand that (comprehensibility); and how much do they rely on F3 formants (the acoustic correspondent of the level of airflow obstruction; accentedness)

Although intelligibility, comprehensibility, and accentedness are crucial to both L+ researchers and language teachers, L+ phonology research can use native production and perception as a baseline against which to measure the effects of specific variables. That is the case of much research on the effects of orthographic forms.

L+ writing systems

This book discusses recent research on another important variable that affects L+ phonology, namely *L+ orthography*, that is to say, the written form of the L+. The present section introduces the basic concepts and terms needed to discuss this issue. It focusses on alphabetic writing systems because these have been the focus of research on OEs on L+ phonology, and it mostly draws examples from English and Italian, as this book is about a study of speakers of these languages.

Writing systems

A spoken language is represented visually using its *writing system*. A writing system has a set of symbols — called *graphemes* — and a set of correspondences that link each symbol to a unit of language. In an alphabetic writing system, a grapheme is a letter or a letter cluster that represents a phoneme. For instance, the English grapheme <th> corresponds to the phoneme /θ/, and vice versa, the phoneme /θ/ corresponds to the grapheme <th>.

Each language has its own writing system — the English writing system, the Italian writing system. Each writing system has a set of correspondences linking graphemes and phonemes: A grapheme-phoneme correspondence (GPC) determines the pronunciation of a grapheme; a phoneme-grapheme correspondence (PGC) determines the spelling of a sound. For instance, the grapheme <th> corresponds to the phoneme /θ/ (a GPC), and the phoneme /θ/ to the grapheme <th> (a PGC). Readers phonologically recode written English (convert it to sounds) using English GPCs, spellers rely on PGCs.

Different writing systems may have the same graphemes — both English and Italian have <n> — or different graphemes; for example, <th> does not exist in the Italian writing system; they may have the same or different GPCs; for instance, in both writing systems, <n> corresponds to /n/, but Italian <ch> corresponds to /k/; in English, it corresponds to /k/ /ʃ/ and /tʃ/ (*chaos, machine, child*) (Bassetti, 2012). Writing systems also have different graphotactics, that is to say, contextual rules. For instance, <d> represents a voiced consonant in German and English, but in German it represents a voiceless consonant in word-final position (a contextual rule). Writing systems also have different degrees of phonological *transparency* (often called *orthographic depth*). A more phonologically transparent, or shallow, writing system has more regular GPCs/PGCs. The Italian writing system is transparent, as one grapheme almost always represents the same phoneme, and vice versa. The English writing system is more phonologically opaque, or deep, because one-to-one correspondences are rare (Carney, 1994).

L+ writing systems

Most L+ learners learn both a language and its writing system; for instance, learners of English$_{L+}$ learn the English writing system as an L+ writing system. The L1 writing system affects how people learn and use their written L+ (Cook & Bassetti, 2005). At a macro level, L+ readers-spellers can rely on processes developed to read and spell their L1. For instance, native users of (transparent) Italian may over-rely on GPCs when reading (opaque) English, because converting graphemes to phonemes is a successful reading strategy in Italian but less so in English. At a micro level, L+ readers-spellers may apply L1 GPCs when reading or spelling L+ sounds and words.

The next chapter discusses how the spelling of L+ sounds and words may affect L+ phonology.

References

Abrahamsson, N., & Hyltenstam, K. (2009). Age of onset and nativelikeness in a second language: Listener perception versus linguistic scrutiny. *Language Learning*, 59(2), 249–306. https://doi.org/10.1111/j.1467-9922.2009.00507.x

Bassetti, B. (2012). Sound and spelling. In C. A. Chapelle (Ed.), *The encyclopedia of applied linguistics* (pp. 5312–5317). Wiley-Blackwell. https://doi.org/10.1002/9781405198431.wbeal1093

Best, C. T., & Tyler, M. D. (2007). Nonnative and second-language speech perception: Commonalities and complementarities. In M. J. Munro & O.-S. Bohn (Eds.), *Language experience in second-language speech learning: In honor of James Emil Flege* (pp. 13–34). John Benjamins.

Carney, E. (1994). *A survey of English spelling*. Routledge.

Colantoni, L., Steele, J., & Escudero, P. (2015). *Second language speech. Theory and practice*. Cambridge University Press.

Cook, V. J. (2016). Premises of multi-competence. In V. J. Cook & L. Wei (Eds.), *The Cambridge handbook of linguistic multi-competence* (pp. 1–25). Cambridge University Press.

Cook, V. J., & Bassetti, B. (2005). An introduction to researching second language writing systems. In V. J. Cook & B. Bassetti (Eds.), *Second language writing systems* (pp. 1–67). Multilingual Matters.

Darcy, I., et al. (2015). Individual differences in L2 acquisition of English phonology: The relation between cognitive abilities and phonological processing. *Learning and Individual Differences*, 40, 63–72. https://doi.org/10.1016/j.lindif.2015.04.005

Derwing, T. M., & Munro, M. J. (2015). *Pronunciation fundamentals. Evidence-based perspectives for L2 teaching and research*. John Benjamins Publishing. https://doi.org/10.1075/lllt.42

Dewaele, J.-M. (2017). Why the dichotomy 'L1 versus LX user' is better than 'native versus non-native speaker'. *Applied Linguistics, 39*(2), 236–240. https://doi.org/10.1093/applin/amw055

Flege, J. E. (1995). Second language speech learning: Theory, findings and problems. In W. Strange (Ed.), *Speech perception and linguistic experience: Theoretical and methodological issues* (pp. 233–277). New York Press.

Flege, J. E., & Bohn, O.-S. (2021). The revised speech learning model (SLM-r). In R. Wayland (Ed.), *Second language speech learning: Theoretical and empirical progress* (pp. 3–83). Cambridge University Press. https://doi.org/10.1017/9781108886901.002

Flege, J. E., & Fletcher, K. L. (1992). Talker and listener effects on degree of perceived foreign accent. *Journal of the Acoustical Society of America, 91*(1), 370–389. https://doi.org/10.1121/1.402780

Iwashita, N., Brown, A., McNamara, T., & O'Hagan, S. (2008). Assessed levels of second language speaking proficiency: How distinct? *Applied Linguistics, 29*(24–49). https://doi.org/10.1093/applin/amm017

Ladefoged, P., & Maddieson, I. (1996). *The sounds of the world's languages*. Blackwell Publishing.

Lee, J., et al. (2015). The effectiveness of second language pronunciation instruction: A meta-analysis. *Applied Linguistics, 36*(3), 345–366.

Levis, J., & Munro, M. J. (2012). Phonetics and phonology: Overview. In Chapelle, C. A. (Ed.), *The encyclopedia of applied linguistics*. https://doi.org/10.1002/9781405198431.wbeal0906

Munro, M. J., & Derwing, T. M. (1995). Foreign accent, comprehensibility, and intelligibility in the speech of second language learners. *Language Learning, 45*(1), 73–97.

Piske, T., et al. (2001). Factors affecting degree of foreign accent in an L2: A review. *Journal of Phonetics, 29*(2), 191–215. https://doi.org/10.1006/jpho.2001.0134

Saito, K., & Plonsky, L. (2019). Effects of second language pronunciation teaching revisited: A proposed measurement framework and meta-analysis. *Language Learning, 69*(3), 652–708. https://doi.org/10.1111/lang.12345

Shively, R. L. (2008). L2 acquisition of [β], [ð] and [ɣ] in Spanish: Impact of experience, linguistic environment, and learner variables. *Southwest Journal of Linguistics, 27*(2), 79.

Suter, R. W. (1976). Predictors of pronunciation accuracy in second language learning. *Language Learning, 26*, 233–253. https://doi.org/10.1111/j.1467-1770.1976.tb00275.x

Vaid, J., Chen, H.-C., & Rao, C. (2022). Biscriptal bilingualism differentially affects segmentation of cross-language homophones: Evidence from Hindi and English users. *International Journal of Bilingualism, 26*(1), 13–30.

Van Leussen, J.-W., & Escudero, P. (2015). Learning to perceive and recognize a second language: The L2LP model revised. *Frontiers in Psychology, 6*, 1000.

2 Effects of orthography on L+ phonology
An overview

Introduction to research on OEs on L+ pronunciation

Acquiring the phonology of a non-native language (plus language, or L+) is notoriously difficult. A factor that has been receiving much attention in the past decade is the effect of L+ orthography on L+ phonology, and research has consistently shown that the orthographic forms — that is to say, the spellings — of L+ sounds and words influence L+ phonological development. Probably the most obvious example is when an L+ speaker pronounces a word 'the way it is written', for instance, producing a [l] in *walk* (Bassetti & Atkinson, 2015). However, OEs are more complicated than that, as L+ speakers know two phonological systems and two orthographic systems that interact, with both positive and negative effects on L+ phonology.

Language teachers have long known that spelling affects L+ pronunciation. Pennington's (1996) introduction to English pronunciation teaching noted that instructed learners' pronunciation is often 'based to a small or large extent on the way words are spelled' (p. 94), and pronunciation dictionaries have long been cautioning learners against so-called 'spelling pronunciations' (Wells, 2000). However, up to the late 2000s, L+ phonology researchers overall believed that orthography was not an important factor. For instance, Flege (2008) wrote: 'Reading seems to have a negligible effect on L+ speech learning, apart from the occasional "spelling" pronunciation of certain words that have been read but never heard' (p. 175). This phonocentric approach among linguists can be traced back to de Saussure's *Course in General Linguistics*, the seminal text that established contemporary linguistics. De Saussure set spoken language as the object of linguistics, replacing the previous focus on written language. He considered the effects of written on spoken language, such as spelling pronunciations, as 'phonetic distortions' caused by 'external factors' (de Saussure, 1915/2013, p. 36). It took researchers a few decades to start researching OEs on phonology.

A brief history of OEs research

In the 1990s and 2000s, occasionally an article would argue that a specific pronunciation error may be due to orthography (for instance, Piske et al.,

DOI: 10.4324/9780429343117-2

2002; Zampini, 1994). The first L+ phonologist to publish a series of papers on OEs was Martha Young-Scholten (Young-Scholten, 1995, 1998, 2002; Young-Scholten & Hannahs, 1997). In 2004, I started presenting papers about the effects of romanised Chinese on pronunciation and phonological awareness in Chinese$_{L+}$ learners. Those were later published as Bassetti (2006, 2007), and in 2006, Young-Scholten invited me to write the first review of the topic, which appeared two years later (Bassetti, 2008). At that point, there was very little peer-reviewed research, and my review included conference abstracts, unpublished reports, and other grey (non-peer-reviewed) literature. I also attempted an explanation of OEs and a list of characteristics, based on current knowledge at the time. Also in 2008, Paola Escudero, Rachel Hayes-Harb, and myself presented papers on L+ phonology at the 'Workshop on the Relation between Orthography and Phonological Acquisition' held in Ghent (Belgium), and two of these were published in the special issue that collected the workshop presentations in 2010 (Escudero & Wanrooij, 2010; Hayes-Harb et al., 2010).

Since then, L+ OEs have rapidly become a hot topic, and there is now a wealth of empirical research (for recent overviews, see Hayes-Harb & Barrios, 2021, who provide detailed descriptions of major studies, and Bassetti, 2024, who provides a roadmap). There is now strong and consistent evidence that orthography affects L+ phonology. Orthographic input can have both positive and negative effects on both speech production and perception.

Facilitative effects of L+ orthographic input

Exposing L+ listeners to written as well as spoken input facilitates them in two ways: It helps them learn more spoken (and written) words, and it improves their perception and production of L+ sounds and words.

Orthographic forms facilitate L+ lexical acquisition

L+ words are easier to learn with orthographic input than without. English$_{L+}$ learners learn more English spoken and written words if they are exposed to their orthographic forms together with their phonological forms — if they read the words' spelling while listening to the words — compared to listening only.

This increase was found at all levels, from beginners, such as US kindergarten children with no English at home (Vadasy & Sanders, 2015) and Chinese (Hu, 2008) and Dutch (Krepel et al., 2021) primary school students, to university students (Bürki et al., 2019). Within the project presented in Chapters 3–5, Cerni et al. (2019) compared high-school students' English$_{L+}$ spoken vocabulary learning with or without word spelling. The students who were exposed to spelling learned more spoken *pseudowords*, that is to say, made-up words created by replacing one sound in a real word, for instance, creating *noppy* from *poppy* (sometimes erroneously called *nonwords* in this line of research). The advantage was found both at the end of the learning cycle and in each of the four learning sessions (see Figure 2.1). Indeed, much research on multimodal input has established that subtitles increase vocabulary acquisition from video (for a review, see Perez, 2022). Interestingly, one study found that auditory and orthographic input result in more vocabulary acquisition than auditory input alone, but not more than orthographic input alone (Uchihara et al., 2022). This is not specific to L+ learners, as word spellings also help English-native children learn more L1 spoken words (Chambrè et al., 2020; Ricketts et al., 2009), including bilingual children (Jubenville et al., 2014). The increase in vocabulary acquisition could be due to the presence of multiple sources of input, including orthographic input, which makes words easier to memorise than auditory input, but part of the effect is due to orthographic forms facilitating L+ speech processing, which is discussed next.

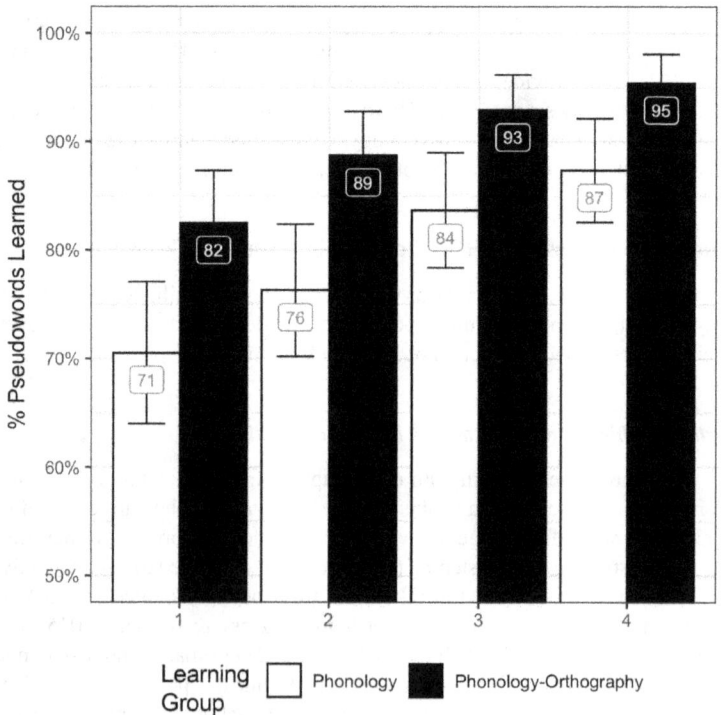

Figure 2.1 Mean percentage of spoken pseudowords learned with and without orthographic input, Cerni et al. (2019).

L+ orthographic forms facilitate the perception and production of L+ sounds and words

Providing orthographic input together with auditory input not only increases lexical acquisition, it also helps learners learn more accurate L+ sounds and word forms.

Much research has investigated how orthographic input helps in receiving and producing a language that learners have never encountered before (a real language or an artificial language created for the study). Participants in these studies are called *L0 learners* in this book, to distinguish them from those who are in the process of actually learning a language (these are usually called 'naïve learners', but L0 is preferred here because it follows the same numbering as L1, L2, L3, and L+, and because 'naïve' has negative connotations, such as 'simple-minded').

Many studies compared L0 word learning with exposure to auditory input alone or to both auditory and orthographic input. In such studies, participants hear a spoken word together with a picture representing its meaning, with or without seeing the word's spelling, and are later tested by looking at the picture and producing or recognising the corresponding word (a measure of their ability to perceive and produce the sounds of the L0). The seminal study by Erdener and Burnham (2005) first demonstrated that L0 learners learn more accurate spoken words with orthographic input than without. Such facilitation has since been found in many studies of L0 learners, with complex consonant clusters (Davidson, 2010), difficult rhotics (Rafat, 2015), and even Chinese lexical tones (Showalter & Hayes-Harb, 2013; tones are variations in pitch level, and are visually represented in romanised Chinese by tone marks, for instance $\bar{i}$ for level-tone [i] and $\grave{i}$ for falling-tone). Research on L0 learning is very important theoretically and methodologically, but the learning processes and strategies adopted to tackle a completely new language during an experimental session may not reflect actual L+ learning and processing. Yet, research has also shown that orthographic input increases accuracy in L+ learning and processing.

Positive effects on L+ speakers were found in various studies by Escudero and colleagues, who studied proficient speakers' discrimination of difficult phonological contrasts using pseudowords (Escudero et al., 2008, 2014; Escudero & Wanrooij, 2010). For instance, Escudero et al. (2008) found that English$_{L+}$ learners learnt English spoken pseudowords containing difficult vowel contrasts and could better discriminate pseudowords if they had been exposed to orthographic input. Other researchers found positive effects, for instance, on German$_{L+}$ vowel length (Nimz & Khattab, 2020), Chinese$_{L+}$ lexical tones (Mok et al., 2018), and Russian$_{L+}$ palatalised consonants (Simonchyk & Darcy, 2018). Orthographic representations can even facilitate the perception of different varieties (Scottish and Australian English$_{L+}$,

Mitterer & McQueen, 2009), including in native speakers (for instance, Canadian English natives' perception of British English, Chambers, 1992). Uchihara et al. (2022), who tested the pronunciation of words learned from reading, listening, or both, found that listening while reading resulted in the best pronunciation, followed by listening, with reading at the bottom. Orthographic input may even improve pronunciation more than phonetic training (vowel pronunciation error correction, Solier et al., 2019) and perception more than visual input (videos of articulators producing the sounds, Pattamadilok et al., 2022). However, orthographic input does not reduce overall accentedness in general.

There is also evidence that L+ learners can use L+ spellings strategically to produce contrasting sounds they cannot discriminate. For instance, Japanese$_{L1}$-English$_{L+}$, who cannot perceive the /l — r/ contrast and cannot distinguish word pairs such as *load-road*, can produce the correct consonant in a word if they know whether the word is spelled with <l> or <r> (Sheldon & Strange, 1982; Eckman, 2004). Similarly, English$_{L1}$-Russian$_{L+}$ learners can rely on spelling to produce a plain or palatalised consonant, which they cannot discriminate.

Orthographic forms result in sound additions, omissions, and substitutions

In spite of its facilitative effects, orthography can also result in the addition, omission, and substitution of sounds in perception, production, and phonological awareness, both in L+s and L0s, with substitutions being the most widely reported phenomenon.

Introduction to the negative effects of orthography on L+ phonology

Orthographic input, by providing a visual and permanent analysis of the auditory input, can facilitate L+/L0 phonological learning and processing compared with auditory input alone. Nonetheless, it can also interfere with the accuracy of perception, production, and awareness, and indeed, some of the same studies that found facilitative effects also found negative ones. Faster L0 word learning was associated with lower accuracy in the pronunciation of the words (Bürki et al., 2019). Escudero, among others, repeatedly reported that orthography facilitated the perception and production of some sounds but interfered with the production of other sounds (Escudero et al., 2014; Escudero & Wanrooij, 2010). Also Nimz & Khattab (2020) reported higher accuracy in vowel duration but lower accuracy in vowel quality, and Uchihara et al. (2022) found higher levels of intelligibility (a positive effect) but also of accentedness (a negative effect).

Addition

Orthography-induced addition — also called *epenthesis* — occurs when L+ speakers add a sound that is present in the orthographic form of a sound or word but not in its phonological form. A typical example is an L+ speaker producing a [b] in *climb* (/klaɪm/, Bassetti & Atkinson, 2015). Additions were also found in L0 learners, who, for instance, produce [kɑməd] with an additional [n] if they learnt the spoken with the spelling <kamand>, but not if they learned the spelling <kamad> or no spelling (Hayes-Harb et al., 2010).

Addition often happens because a letter belongs to a larger orthographic unit, such as a multi-letter grapheme, or a morphemic spelling. Such multi-letter graphemes include, for example, <ng> representing /ŋ/ in *king* and <al> representing /ɔ:/ in *walk* (letters such as <g> and <l> are often called 'silent letters'). Another example is the discontinuous grapheme <V__e>, where a final letter <e> marks the preceding vowel as a long vowel, for instance, <a__e> in *made* /meɪd/. Because of these multi-letter graphemes, L+ speakers add consonants such as [g] in *king* (Cabanero & Alves, 2008) and [l] in *walk* (Bassetti & Atkinson, 2015) and add a vowel corresponding to the final <-e> at the end of words such as *made* (Silveira, 2007). Orthography-induced addition has also been found in L0 learners perceiving (Hayes-Harb et al., 2010), producing (Rafat & Stevenson, 2019), and segmenting (Detey & Nespoulous, 2008), that is to say, dividing into sounds, newly learned L0 words. Other than with multi-letter graphemes, addition can also happen when L+ speakers phonologically recode (convert to sound) a multi-letter morphemic spelling letter-by-letter. For instance, the English past-tense marker <-ed> often represents a consonant ([t] after a voiceless consonant or [d] after a voiced consonant or a vowel) and only represents /ɪd/ after [t] or [d]. Because of the spelling <ed>, English$_{L+}$ speakers often add a vowel and produce [Vd] (Bassetti & Atkinson, 2015).

The relationship between orthography and sound addition can also be indirect, that is to say, it may be due to exposure to orthographic forms rather than being caused directly by recoding a grapheme into an extra sound. For instance, those who learn complex spoken consonant clusters often omit consonants in production, but if also exposed to orthographic input, they often retain all the consonants they have seen in the spelling and add epenthetic vowels to make consonant sequences pronounceable. This addition was found in the production of consonant clusters in Polish$_{L0}$ words (Young-Scholten et al., 1999, 2002), and in the awareness of French$_{L+}$ learners, who counted one more syllable in pseudowords they had seen in writing as a consequence of vowel addition (Detey & Nespoulous, 2008).

Omission

Orthography-induced omissions occur when L+ learners omit a sound that is present in a word's phonological form but not in its orthographic form. Evidence is far less common than additions or substitutions, but an example can be found in learners of Chinese$_{L+}$. Romanised Chinese (a roman alphabet transcription used for language teaching), which is used for teaching, represents Chinese triphthongs in two ways. In syllables with no initial consonant, triphthongs are spelled with three letters, and learners produce and categorise them as triphthongs. For instance, [jou] is spelled <you>, and learners produce [jou] and count and segment three vowels in metalinguistic awareness tasks. In syllables with an initial consonant, the triphthong is spelled with two letters, for instance, [ljou] is spelled <liu>. L+ learners produce a diphthong, usually [ju], and count and segment only two vowels (Bassetti, 2006, 2007; Pytlyk, 2017; for L0 learners, see Pytlyk, 2011; note that this happens in the absence of alphabetic input (for instance, when seeing Chinese characters).

Substitution

Orthography-induced substitutions occur when L+ speakers perceive or produce a sound other than the target one because of its written representation. These are the most commonly reported negative OEs in the literature.

An early study by Young-Scholten (2004) found that English$_{L1}$-German$_{L+}$ beginner learners replace word-final voiceless consonants with their voiced counterparts, because such consonants are spelled with a grapheme that represents a voiced consonant both in English$_{L1}$ and in other (word-initial and medial) positions in German$_{L+}$. Learners therefore produce [d] instead of [t] in word-final position, where [t] is spelled <D>, for instance, producing [kɪnd] as *[kɪnd] because it is spelled <Kind>. This is because <d> represents [d] both in English$_{L1}$ and in other positions in German$_{L+}$. Similarly, Young-Scholten and Langer (2015) later reported that German$_{L+}$ beginners also replace word-initial [z] with [s] because of its spelling <s>.

The most commonly reported cause of sound substitution is an incongruence between the GPCs of the L1 and the target language, that is to say, that the same grapheme represents different sounds in the two languages. This is often found in research on L0s. For instance, Barrios and Hayes-Harb (2020) created an artificial language modelled on German and found that learners substituted word-final voiceless consonants with voiced counterparts because of consonant spelling, replicating what Young-Scholten (2004) had found with German$_{L+}$ learners. The orthographic nature of these effects is evident from another study by Hayes-Harb and colleagues (Hayes-Harb & Cheng, 2016), who found sound substitutions in English$_{L1}$ learners of Chinese$_{L0}$ pseudowords who had been exposed to romanised Chinese spellings but not in those only exposed to auditory forms due to incongruences between the GPCs of English and romanised Chinese. Substitutions have been reported in a variety of L0s, for instance Mathieu (2016) investigated Arabic$_{L0}$, and found that English$_{L1}$ speakers who had only received auditory input outperformed peers also exposed to orthographic forms because the same graphemes represented different sounds in Arabic$_{L0}$ and English$_{L1}$. Arabic$_{L0}$. It appears that L- learners, faced with the phonology and orthography of a language for the first time, rely on L0 orthographic forms and phonologically recode them using L1 GPCs.

Looking beyond first exposure to a language, orthography-induced sound substitutions are also found in L+ learners and speakers, including advanced L+ learners (Escudero et al., 2014; Hayes-Harb et al., 2018). Looking at perception, Shea (2017) found that English$_{L1}$ listeners were more likely to perceive a Spanish$_{L+}$ approximant as a stop if they saw the word's spelling, where the consonant is spelled with a letter that represents a stop in English$_{L1}$, for instance, perceiving [b] instead of [β] in [kaβejo] ('hair') because of its spelling <cabello>. Looking at production, advanced speakers of American English$_{L+}$ produce [t] and [d] instead of the flaps produced by native speakers because these consonants are spelled as <t, d, d, dd> (Vokic, 2011). Most studies investigated perception or production, but one study revealed orthography-induced substitutions in metalinguistic awareness, showing that French GPCs result in vowel substitutions when French$_{L1}$-English$_{L+}$ speakers adapt English pseudowords to be used as loanwords in French$_{L1}$, but only if they are exposed to the words' spellings in addition to the spoken words (Vendelin & Peperkamp, 2006).

OEs are not only caused by incongruences between the GPCs of the L1 and the L0/L+ but can also happen because L+ speakers ignore L+ GPCs, graphotactics (contextual rules), or lexical spellings. A series of studies by Bassetti and colleagues investigated OEs on English vowels in Italian$_{L1}$ speakers of English$_{L+}$. Italians generally cannot perceive the qualitative differences between English lax and tense vowels, such as [ɪ]-[iː], but produce them as short and long vowels, respectively ([i]-[iː]), and rely on orthographic forms to determine vowel length. They apply a successful 'vowel digraph = long vowel' correspondence but also overextend a 'single vowel letter = short vowel' correspondence to words where it does not apply. They therefore produce the same English$_{L+}$ tense vowel as a long vowel when it is spelled with a digraph, or as a short vowel when it is spelled with a single letter, zero letters, or the grapheme <V_e> (where the final <-e> marks the preceding vowel as long), for instance, substituting [i] to [iː] in *ski* but not in *see*, and in *scene* but not in *seen* (Bassetti & Atkinson, 2015; Bassetti et al., 2018, 2020, 2021).

The evidence reviewed earlier shows that the sound that is substituted can be a different L+ sound, an allophone of the L+ sound, (rarely) an L1 sound, or a sound in-between an L1 and an L+ sound, as follows:

Different L+ sounds. German$_{L+}$ beginners substitute [d] for [t] and [s] for [z] (Young-Scholten, 2004; Young-Scholten & Langer, 2015), and Italian$_{L1}$ English$_{L+}$ learners occasionally produce <w> as [v] in words such as *wood* or *water* (Bassetti & Atkinson, 2015).

Allophones of the L+ sound. For instance, American English$_{L+}$ speakers produce <t> and <d> as [t] or [d] in contexts where native speakers produce flaps (Vokic, 2011), and Korean$_{L+}$ learners produce different variants of Korean [h] if they see different consonant spellings during word learning (Han & Kim, 2017).

L1 sounds. Substitutions with an L1 sound are probably rare. Zampini (1994) found that English$_{L1}$ beginner Spanish$_{L+}$ learners produced [v] in Spanish$_{L+}$ words spelled with <v>, because of the English correspondence <v> = [v]. The consonant [v] is not attested in Spanish.

L1-L+ in-between sounds. The outcome sound can reflect complex interactions between the orthographies and the phonologies of the L1 and the L+. For instance, Polish$_{L1}$ learners produce German$_{L+}$ [oː] close to Polish [ɔ] if spelled <o> (which in Polish$_{L1}$ represents [ɔ]), or close to Polish [u] if not exposed to spelling; the outcome sound is in-between the vowels of the two languages (Nimz & Khattab, 2020).

To summarise, there is much evidence that orthographic forms consistently result in sound substitutions across languages.

Final remarks on the categorisation of OEs

The categorisation of additions, omissions, and substitutions is useful to describe OEs. For instance, when English$_{L+}$ speakers produce the <ed> in *talked* as [Vd] instead of [t] (Bassetti & Atkinson, 2015), this production can be described as an addition (a vowel) and a substitution ([d] for [t]). This categorisation is economical, as only three categories can describe all OEs. For instance, Rafat and Stevenson (2019) report that English$_{L1}$ Spanish$_{L0}$ learners produce [pojo] as [poljo] because of the spelling <pollo> and describe this production as an 'auditory-orthographic integration' (p. 427), with the 'combination sound' [lj] resulting from the integration of the auditory input [j] and the L1 sound [l] (that originated from phonologically recoding <ll> as [l]). A simpler alternative is to describe [poljo] as the outcome of an addition ([l] added to the phonological word [pojo]). While different descriptions may reflect different researchers' interpretations of the cause of the observed OE, this tripartite categorisation is an economical solution.

The cause of OEs: The L+ user's orthographic knowledge

Additions, omissions, and substitutions are ultimately caused by inconsistencies between the L+ orthographic knowledge of L+ learners and users — what they know about the L+ writing system — and how the L+ writing system actually works. Orthographic knowledge includes grapheme-phoneme correspondences (how graphemes are phonologically recoded) and phoneme-grapheme correspondences (how phonemes are encoded, that is to say, spelled), as well as graphotactics, which determines the context where GPCs apply. Most L+ speakers encounter the L+ after having established both an L1 phonological system, which affects how they perceive L+ sounds and phonological contrasts, and L1 orthographic knowledge, which affects how they establish L+ GPCs and phonotactics. Their orthographic knowledge may differ from a native user's orthographic knowledge as follows:

Unfamiliar GPCs. L+ learners and users sometimes do not know an L+ GPC. For instance, not knowing that <augh> represents /ɔ:/ in *caught* may result in adding [g], and ignoring that <al> represents /ɔ:/ in *walk* may result in adding [l] (Bassetti & Atkinson, 2015). Ignoring that <V__e> (so-called 'silent e') represents a long V may result in producing and perceiving a short V, for instance, in *scene* but not in *seen* (Bassetti et al., 2020, 2021).

L1-influenced unattested GPCs. L+ learners/users establish unattested GPCs (that are not present in native speakers' orthographic knowledge). These are often caused by an incongruence between the GPCs of their L1 and L+ (see Substitution presented earlier).

Novel unattested GPCs. Less frequently, an unattested GPC may be an original creation of the L+ user that cannot be explained in terms of either L1 or L+ GPCs, such as producing <ght> as [tʃ] in *caught* (Bassetti & Atkinson, 2015). This may be due to limited knowledge of the target sound or word, or perhaps it may be caused by GPCs in languages other than L1 and L+ that the L+ user may know.

Graphotactic rules. Graphotactics determines the contexts in which a GPC applies. Not knowing that <mb> represents /m/ in English word-final position (<mb#>=/m/) results in adding [b] in *lamb* (Bassetti & Atkinson, 2015), and not knowing that <b, d, g> represent voiceless /p, t, k/ in German word-final position (for instance, <b#>=/p/) results in substituting /p, t, k/ with [b, d, g] (Young-Scholten, 2004).

Overgeneralised GPCs. L+ learners may not know the phonological form of a word, and incorrectly recode the orthographic form by overgeneralising an L+ GPC that does not apply to that word. For instance, if they do not know the spoken word [kɔ:t], they may phonologically recode *caught* with a [f], because <augh>=[f] is an English GPC, but not in this word. This results in the production of a spoken word that would not have existed in the absence of orthographic input.

Multiple causes. Finally, the same production may have multiple causes, or it may be impossible to know which of the many potential causes is having an effect. English$_{L1}$ speakers who substitute voiceless [t] with voiced [d] in German$_{L+}$ words ending in <d> may ignore the graphotactic rule that word-final <d> represents /t/, may be overgeneralising the German GPC <d>=/t/, may be influenced by the English GPC <d>=/t/, or may be affected by more than one of these causes. Such an effect can be ascribed to more than one cause, and may be the outcome of multiple causes.

To summarise, L+ orthographic knowledge determines how L+ learners/users phonologically recode the orthographic forms of L+ sounds and words. This in turn affects their L+ phonological system (the set of L+ sounds and phonological contrasts in their mind) and L+ phonological lexicon (the 'mental vocabulary', or set of mental representations of L+ words in their mind).

Null results and variability

The evidence that orthography affects phonology is strong and consistent, but a few studies found no effects. Furthermore, the literature reveals high levels of variability, meaning that not all L+ speakers and not all items (sounds or words) are equally affected by orthography.

Null results

Some studies found no effects of orthographic input.

With L0 learners, orthography does not help if the to-be-learned sound or phonological contrast is too difficult to perceive. This was neatly demonstrated by Escudero (2015). This study compared English$_{L1}$ speakers' learning of easy or difficult Dutch$_{L0}$ phonological contrasts. Orthographic input facilitated the acquisition of contrasting sounds that participants were able to distinguish but had no effect on those they could not perceive. Other studies also show that orthography cannot help with difficult L0 phonological contrasts, for instance Arabic$_{L0}$ velar-uvular contrasts (Showalter & Hayes-Harb, 2015). Orthography does not help if L0 learners are not exposed enough to the sounds and/or symbols of the L0. This is the most likely explanation for the null results in various studies, such as Pytlyk (2011), who found no OEs, and Mathieu (2016), who found better learning without than with orthographic input in written Arabic, which was new to participants. In some cases, the lack of OEs may simply be due to small sample sizes (a possible example is Simon et al., 2010).

Among L+ learners, when predicted OEs are not found, this is often due to L1 phonology. For instance, Hayes-Harb and Hacking (2015), who found that lexical stress marks do not help English$_{L1}$ learners learn stress position in Russian$_{L+}$ words, argued that these learners do not pay attention to word stress because it is not salient in English$_{L1}$. Young-Scholten argued that learners beyond the early stages do not apply L1 GPCs if the L+ sound is a new phonological category that has no corresponding L1 category. This would explain why, over time, English$_{L1}$ learners recode German <z> as /tʃ/ (Young-Scholten & Langer, 2015) and <ch> as a velar fricative (Young-Scholten, 2004), rather than recoding as /z/ and /ʃ/ respectively, as in English$_{L1}$.

Variability and predictors of OEs

Together with strong evidence of OEs, the literature reveals a huge level of variability. This means that there must be variables that modulate OEs — characteristics of the individual, the target item (the spoken or written form of sounds or words), and the task. Variables that impact L+ phonology (see Variables Affecting L+ Phonology) are likely to impact OEs on L+ phonology too, and there may be orthography-specific variables, such as level of literacy or type of writing system.

At present, these variables have not been systematically investigated; evidence comes from small-scale studies and is limited, inconsistent, and unreliable. A few solid findings are reported here.

Individual-level predictors

L1 writing system. Orthography affects native users of transparent writing systems more than native users of opaque ones. Among L0 learners, this was established by Erdener and Burnham's (2005) comparison of (transparent) Turkish$_{L1}$ and (opaque) English$_{L1}$ L0 learners, and confirmed by later studies, for instance Ijalba and Obler's (2015) comparison of Spanish and English natives. Still, native users of opaque writing systems are also affected, as shown in the various studies of English natives reported earlier (for an exception, see the Farsi natives in Rafat et al., 2021).

OEs were found in native users of non-alphabetic L1 writing systems (Chinese$_{L1}$, Han & Kim, 2017; Korean$_{L1}$, Mok et al., 2018). A replication on Chinese$_{L1}$-English$_{L+}$ speakers (Deng et al., 2022) found the same additions and substitutions as in Italian natives (Bassetti & Atkinson, 2015).

L+ writing system. Learners may rely more on L+ orthographic forms if the L+ is phonologically transparent than if it has irregular GPCs. With L0s, this was first reported by Erdener and Burnham (2005) and confirmed in later studies (Ijalba & Obler, 2015), but effects were also found when the level of transparency was unclear to learners (Hayes-Harb et al., 2018). With L+ speakers, the situation is unclear, as Solier et al. (2019) found OEs on (opaque) French$_{L+}$, but Zhang et al. (2021) found none on Chinese$_{L+}$, even though the individual to-be-learned characters were transparent.

Age of onset of bilingualism. There are no OEs in L+ speakers who learnt the L+ as children in an L+ environment, such as English$_{L+}$ early bilinguals in the United States (Carrasco-Ortiz et al., 2019) and Malta (Mitterer, 2021), although one study found OEs in production (but not perception) among Spanish-Basque early bilinguals (Stoehr & Martin, 2022). The absence of OEs is probably due to having acquired both phonological systems early in life.

Exposure to spoken and written input. The role of naturalistic exposure is worth investigating, although Young-Scholten and Langer (2015) found no link between OEs and length of residence in three naturalistic adult learners. A small-scale study by Young-Scholten (2002) tested whether the amount of exposure to L+ orthographic input was linked to stronger OEs, but this requires further investigation.

Item-level predictors

At the level of sound and grapheme, a crucial factor is the congruence between L1 and L+ GPCs. As discussed at length in Substitution, incongruent GPCs — where the same grapheme represents different sounds in the L1 and L+ — can result in substitutions, and congruent GPCs — where the same grapheme represents the same phoneme — can have a facilitative effect.

The perceptual difficulty of the L+ sound, or phonological contrast, also modulates OEs. OEs are stronger when L+ sounds are easier to perceive; for instance, marking palatisation in spelling facilitates its perception within the word, but not in word-final position, where it is less salient (Simonchyk & Darcy, 2018). At least with L0s, if a sound or phonological contrast is difficult to perceive, orthography cannot help (Escudero, 2015; Showalter & Hayes-Harb, 2015).

Among other possible factors, one study found effects of word class, as English$_{L+}$ <ng> was correctly realised as [ŋ] in verbs with the suffix -*ing* and as [ng] in content words (Cabanero & Alves, 2008).

Task-level predictors

Orthographic input. It has been argued that OEs may be stronger in tasks that provide orthographic input, such as oral reading. Orthographic input is not necessary for OEs to occur, as most of the studies reported earlier found OEs in purely oral tasks, showing that OEs are not an artifact of presenting orthographic forms. Yet it is unclear whether the presence of orthographic input reinforces OEs. Some studies compared the same learners performing the same task with auditory and orthographic input or with auditory input alone, and found stronger OEs with orthographic input; for instance, Bassetti and Atkinson's (2015) comparison of reading aloud and sentence repetition, and Özçelik and Sprouse's (2016) study of L+ vowels presented auditorily and orthographically or auditorily only. Another potentially relevant variable is the level of formality of the task, but there is very limited research on OEs in spontaneous production (but see Young-Scholten & Langer, 2015) or on comparisons of the same OE in different tasks.

Phonological process. An interesting question is whether tasks tapping different processes find similar effects. There seems to be a link between production and awareness: Bassetti found the same omission in the production (Bassetti, 2006) and segmentation (Bassetti, 2007) of Chinese$_{L+}$ vowels in

Italian$_{L1}$ learners. However, the results are not conclusive because the two studies had different participants. Other studies found that effects appear in awareness but not in speech production. The early bilinguals in Piske et al. (2002), who had acquired English$_{L+}$ in a naturalistic context from age seven, produced targetlike vowels in English words but showed OEs in a task where they had to create a pseudoword by inserting a vowel in a spoken disyllabic frame ([b_do]), producing an L1 vowel in such L+ pseudowords. Such a complex task may require an orthographic strategy, which is not representative of these bilinguals' normal L+ speech production. Stoehr and Martin (2022) found orthography-induced substitutions in perception (a lexical decision task) but not in reading aloud in early bilinguals. It is possible that the same orthographic form affects some aspects of L+ phonology but not others.

Conclusions

In conclusion, although there is interest in variables that may modulate OEs, research is limited, often underpowered, and rarely replicated. The role of such variables is one of the issues addressed in the project reported in the following chapters.

References

Barrios, S. L., & Hayes-Harb, R. (2020). Second language learning of phonological alternations with and without orthographic input: Evidence from the acquisition of a German-like voicing alternation. *Applied Psycholinguistics, 41*(3), 517–545. https://doi.org/10.1017/S0142716420000077

Bassetti, B. (2006). Orthographic input and phonological representations in learners of Chinese as a Foreign Language. *Written Language and Literacy, 9*(1), 95–114. https://doi.org/10.1075/wll.9.1.07bas

Bassetti, B. (2007). Effects of hanyu pinyin on pronunciation in learners of Chinese as a Foreign Language. In A. Guder, X. Jiang, & Y. Wan (Eds.), *The cognition, learning and teaching of Chinese characters* (pp. 155–179). Beijing Language and Culture University Press.

Bassetti, B. (2008). Orthographic input and second language phonology. In T. Piske & M. Young-Scholten (Eds.), *Input matters in SLA* (pp. 191–206). Multilingual Matters. https://doi.org/10.21832/9781847691118-013

Bassetti, B. (2024). Orthographic effects in the phonetics and phonology of second language learners and users. In M. Amengual (Ed.), *The Cambridge handbook of bilingual phonetics and phonology*. Cambridge University Press.

Bassetti, B., & Atkinson, N. (2015). Effects of orthographic forms on pronunciation in experienced instructed second language learners. *Applied Psycholinguistics, 36*, 67–91. https://doi.org/10.1017/S0142716414000435

Bassetti, B., Mairano, P., Masterson, J., & Cerni, T. (2020). Effects of orthographic forms on L2 speech production and phonological awareness, with consideration of speaker-level predictors. *Language Learning, 70*(4), 1218–1256. https://doi.org/10.1111/lang.12423

Bassetti, B., Masterson, J., Cerni, T., & Mairano, P. (2021). Orthographic forms affect speech perception in a second language: Consonant and vowel length in L2 English. *Journal of Experimental Psychology: Human Perception and Performance, 47*(12), 1583–1603. https://doi.org/10.1037/xhp0000949

Bassetti, B., Sokolović-Perović, M., Mairano, P., & Cerni, T. (2018). Orthography-induced length contrasts in the second language phonological systems of L2 speakers of English: Evidence from minimal pairs. *Language and Speech, 61*(4), 577–597. https://doi.org/10.1177/0023830918780141

Bürki, A., et al. (2019). Orthography and second language word learning: Moving beyond "friend or foe?". *The Journal of the Acoustical Society of America, 145*(4), 265–271. https://doi.org/10.1121/1.5094923

Cabanero, M. B., & Alves, U. K. (2008). A transferência grafo-fônico-fonológica na produção de seqüências ortográficas 'ng' do inglês (L2): uma abordagem conexionista. *ReVEL, 6*(11).

Carrasco-Ortiz, H., et al. (2019). Cross-language effects of phonological and orthographic similarity in cognate word recognition: The role of language dominance. *Linguistic approaches to bilingualism.* https://doi.org/10.1075/lab.18095.car

Cerni, T., et al. (2019). Effects of orthographic forms on the acquisition of novel spoken words in a second language. *Frontiers in Communication, 4*(31). https://doi.org/10.3389/fcomm.2019.00031

Chambers, J. K. (1992). Dialect acquisition. *Language, 68*(4), 673–705. https://doi.org/10.2307/416850

Chambrè, S. J., et al. (2020). Phonological decoding enhances orthographic facilitation of vocabulary learning in first graders. *Reading and Writing, 33*(5), 1133–1162. https://doi.org/10.1007/s11145-019-09997-w

Davidson, L. (2010). Phonetic bases of similarities in cross-language production: Evidence from English and Catalan. *Journal of Phonetics, 38*(2), 272–288. https://doi.org/10.1016/j.wocn.2010.01.001

de Saussure, F. (1915/2013). *Course in general linguistics* (R. Harris, Trans.). Bloomsbury.

Deng, W., Chan, K. Y., & Au Yeung, K. M. (2022). Orthographic effects on L2 production and L2 proficiency in ESL learners with non-alphabetic and orthographically opaque L1. *Applied Psycholinguistics, 43*(6), 1329–1357. https://doi.org/10.1017/S014271642200039X

Detey, S., & Nespoulous, J.-L. (2008). Can orthography influence second language syllabic segmentation? Japanese epenthetic vowels and French consonantal clusters. *Lingua, 118*(1), 66–81. https://doi.org/10.1016/j.lingua.2007.04.003

Eckman, F. R. (2004). From phonemic differences to constraint rankings: Research on second language phonology. *Studies in Second Language Acquisition, 26*, 513–549.

Erdener, V. D., & Burnham, D. K. (2005). The role of audiovisual speech and orthographic information in nonnative speech production. *Language Learning, 55*(2), 191–228. https://doi.org/10.1111/j.0023-8333.2005.00303.x

Escudero, P. (2015). Orthography plays a limited role when learning the phonological forms of new words: The case of Spanish and English learners of novel Dutch words. *Applied Psycholinguistics, 36*(01), 7–22. https://doi.org/10.1017/S014271641400040X

Escudero, P., & Wanrooij, K. (2010). The effect of L1 orthography on non-native vowel perception. *Language and Speech, 53*(3), 343–365. https://doi.org/10.1177/0023830910371447

Escudero, P., et al. (2008). Novel second-language words and asymmetric lexical access. *Journal of Phonetics, 36*(2), 345–360. https://doi.org/10.1016/j.wocn.2007.11.002

Escudero, P., et al. (2014). Learning words in a new language: Orthography doesn't always help. *Bilingualism: Language and Cognition, 17,* 384–395. https://doi.org/10.1017/s1366728913000436

Flege, J. E. (2008). Give input a chance! In T. Piske & M. Young-Scholten (Eds.), *Input matters in SLA* (pp. 175–190). Multilingual Matters. https://doi.org/10.21832/9781847691118-013

Han, J.-I., & Kim, J.-Y. (2017). The influence of orthography on the production of alphabetic, second-language allophones by speakers of a non-alphabetic language. *Journal of Psycholinguistic Research, 46*(4), 963–982. https://doi.org/10.1007/s10936-016-9474-7

Hayes-Harb, R., & Barrios, S. (2021). The influence of orthography in second language phonological acquisition. *Language Teaching,* 1–30. https://doi.org/10.1017/S0261444820000658

Hayes-Harb, R., & Cheng, H.-W. (2016). The influence of the *pinyin* and *zhuyin* writing systems on the acquisition of Mandarin word forms by native English speakers. *Frontiers in Psychology, 7.* https://doi.org/10.3389/fpsyg.2016.00785

Hayes-Harb, R., & Hacking, J. (2015). The influence of written stress marks on native English speakers' acquisition of Russian lexical stress. *Slavic and East European Journal, 59*(1), 91–109. https://doi.org/10.30851/59.1.005

Hayes-Harb, R., et al. (2010). Learning the phonological forms of new words: Effects of orthographic and auditory input. *Language and Speech, 53*(3), 367–381. https://doi.org/10.1177/0023830910371460

Hayes-Harb, R., et al. (2018). Orthographic input and the acquisition of German final devoicing by native speakers of English. *Language and Speech, 61*(4), 547–564. https://doi.org/10.1177/0023830917710048

Hu, C.-F. (2008). Use orthography in L2 auditory word learning: Who benefits? *Reading and Writing, 21*(8), 823–841. https://doi.org/10.1007/s11145-007-9094-6

Ijalba, E., & Obler, L. K. (2015). *First language grapheme-phoneme transparency effects in adult Second-language learning. Reading in a Foreign Language, 27*(1), 47–70. https://doi.org/ 10125/66700

Jubenville, K., et al. (2014). The moderating effect of orthographic consistency on oral vocabulary learning in monolingual and bilingual children. *Journal of Experimental Child Psychology, 126,* 245–263. https://doi.org/10.1016/j.jecp.2014.05.002

Krepel, A., et al. (2021). Does the availability of orthography support L2 word learning? *Reading and Writing, 34*(2), 467–496. https://doi.org/10.1007/s11145-020-10078-6

Mathieu, L. (2016). The influence of foreign scripts on the acquisition of a second language phonological contrast. *Second Language Research, 32*(2), 145–170. https://doi.org/10.1177/0267658315601882

Mitterer, H. (2021). The role of orthography in learning a second language: Evidence from Maltese English. *Xjenza Online, 9*(3), 162–172. https://doi.org/10.7423/XJENZA.2021.3.09

Mitterer, H., & McQueen, J. M. (2009). Foreign subtitles help but native-language subtitles harm foreign speech perception. *PloS one, 4*(11), e7785. https://doi.org/10.1371/journal.pone.0007785

Mok, P. P. K., et al. (2018). Orthographic effects on the perception and production of L2 Mandarin tones. *Speech Communication, 101,* 1–10. https://doi.org/10.1016/j.specom.2018.05.002

Nimz, K., & Khattab, G. (2020). On the role of orthography in L2 vowel production: The case of Polish learners of German. *Second Language Research, 4*(36), 623–652. https://doi.org/10.1177/0267658319828424

Özçelik, Ö., & Sprouse, R. A. (2016). Decreasing dependence on orthography in phonological development: Evidence from vowel harmony in English-Turkish interlanguage. In A. E. Gürel (Ed.), *Second language acquisition of Turkish* (pp. 49–72). John Benjamins. https://doi.org/10.1075/lald.59.03ozc

Pattamadilok, C., Welby, P., & Tyler, M. D. (2022). The contribution of visual articulatory gestures and orthography to speech processing: Evidence from novel word learning. *Journal of Experimental Psychology: Learning, Memory, and Cognition, 48*(10), 1542–1558. https://doi.org/10.1037/xlm0001036

Pennington, M. C. (1996). *Phonology in English language teaching*. Longman.

Perez, M. M. (2022). Second or foreign language learning through watching audio-visual input and the role of on-screen text. *Language Teaching, 55*(2), 163–192. https://doi.org/10.1017/S0261444821000501

Piske, T., et al. (2002). The production of English vowels by fluent early and late Italian-English bilinguals. *Phonetica, 59*, 49–71. https://doi.org/10.1159/000056205

Pytlyk, C. (2011). Shared orthography: Do shared written symbols influence the perception of L2 sounds? *Modern Language Journal, 54*(4), 541–557. https://doi.org/10.1111/j.1540-4781.2011.01244.x

Pytlyk, C. (2017). Are orthographic effects language specific? The influence of second language orthography on second language phoneme awareness. *Applied Psycholinguistics, 38*(2), 233–262. https://doi.org/10.1017/S0142716416000175

Rafat, Y. (2015). The interaction of acoustic and orthographic input in the acquisition of Spanish assibilated/fricative rhotics. *Applied Psycholinguistics, 36*(01), 43–66. https://doi.org/10.1017/S0142716414000423

Rafat, Y., & Stevenson, R. A. (2019). Auditory-orthographic integration at the onset of L2 speech acquisition. *Language and Speech, 62*(3), 427–451. https://doi.org/10.1177/0023830918777537

Rafat, Y., et al. (2021). First-language-specific orthographic effects in second-language speech: A comparison of Korean–English and Farsi–English bilinguals. *Journal of Monolingual and Bilingual Speech, 3*(1), 102–122. https://doi.org/10.1558/jmbs.15682

Ricketts, J., et al. (2009). Orthographic facilitation in oral vocabulary acquisition. *Quarterly Journal of Experimental Psychology, 62*(10), 1948–1966. https://doi.org/10.1080/17470210802696104

Shea, C. (2017). L1 English/L2 Spanish: Orthography–phonology activation without contrasts. *Second Language Research, 33*(2), 207–232. https://doi.org/10.1177/0267658316684905

Sheldon, A., & Strange, W. (1982). The acquisition of /l/ and /r/ by Japanese learners of English: Evidence that speech production can precede speech perception. *Applied Psycholinguistics, 3*, 243–261.

Showalter, C. E., & Hayes-Harb, R. (2013). Unfamiliar orthographic information and second language word learning: A novel lexicon study. *Second Language Research, 29*(2), 185–200. https://doi.org/10.1177/0267658313480154

Showalter, C. E., & Hayes-Harb, R. (2015). Native English speakers learning Arabic: The influence of novel orthographic information on second language phonological acquisition. *Applied Psycholinguistics, 36*(01), 23–42. https://doi.org/10.1017/S0142716414000411

Silveira, R. (2007). The role of task-type and orthography in the production of word-final consonants. *Revista de Estudos da Linguagem, 15*(1), 143–176.

Simon, E., Chambless, D., & Alves, U. K. (2010). Understanding the role of orthography in the acquisition of a non-native vowel contrast. *Language Sciences, 32*(3), 380–394. https://doi.org/10.1016/j.langsci.2009.07.001

Simonchyk, A., & Darcy, I. (2018). The effect of orthography on the lexical encoding of palatalized consonants in L2 Russian. *Language and Speech, 61*(4), 522–546. https://doi.org/10.1177/0023830918761490

Solier, C., et al. (2019). Written training tasks are better than oral training tasks at improving L2 learners' speech production. *Applied Psycholinguistics, 40*(6), 1455–1480. https://doi.org/10.1017/S014271641900033X

Stoehr, A., & Martin, C. D. (2022). Orthography affects L1 and L2 speech perception but not production in early bilinguals. *Bilingualism: Language and Cognition, 25*(1), 108–120. https://doi.org/10.1017/S1366728921000523

Uchihara, T., Webb, S., Saito, K., & Trofimovich, P. (2022). Does mode of input affect how second language learners create form–meaning connections and pronounce second language words? *The Modern Language Journal, 106*(2), 351–370. https://doi.org/10.1111/modl.12775

Vadasy, P. F., & Sanders, E. A. (2015). Incremental learning of difficult words in story contexts: The role of spelling and pronouncing new vocabulary. *Reading and Writing, 28*(3), 371–394. https://doi.org/10.1007/s11145-014-959-9

Vendelin, I., & Peperkamp, S. (2006). The influence of orthography on loanword adaptations. *Lingua, 116*(7), 996–1007. https://doi.org/10.1016/j.lingua.2005.07.005

Vokic, G. (2011). When alphabets collide: Alphabetic first-language speakers' approach to speech production in an alphabetic second language. *Second Language Research, 27*(3), 391–417. https://doi.org/10.1177/0267658310396627

Wells, J. C. (2000). *Longman pronunciation dictionary*. Pearson Education.

Young-Scholten, M. (1995). The negative effects of positive evidence on L2 phonology. In L. Eubank, L. Selinker, & M. Sharwood Smith (Eds.), *The current state of interlanguage*. Benjamins.

Young-Scholten, M. (1998). Second language syllable simplification: Deviant development or deviant input? In J. Allan & J. Leather (Eds.), *New sounds '97* (pp. 351–360). University of Amsterdam.

Young-Scholten, M. (2002). Orthographic input in L2 phonological development. In P. Burmeister, T. Piske, & A. Rohde (Eds.), *An integrated view of language development: Papers in honour of Henning Wode* (pp. 263–279). Wissenschaftlicher Verlag Trier.

Young-Scholten, M. (2004). Prosodic constraints on allophonic distribution in adult L2 acquisition. *International Journal of Bilingualism, 8*(1), 67–77. https://doi.org/10.1177/13670069040080010501

Young-Scholten, M., & Hannahs, S. S. (1997). Current issues in the first and second language acquisition of phonology. In S. S. Hannahs & M. Young-Scholten (Eds.), *Focus on phonological acquisition* (pp. 1–14). John Benjamins.

Young-Scholten, M., & Langer, M. (2015). The role of orthographic input in second language German: Evidence from naturalistic adult learners' production. *Applied Psycholinguistics, 36*(1), 93–114. https://doi.org/10.1017/s0142716414000447

Young-Scholten, M., et al. (1999). Focus on form in phonology: Orthographic exposure as a promoter of epenthesis. In P. Robinson & N. O. Jungheim (Eds.), *Pragmatics and pedagogy. Proceedings of the third PacSLRF* (Vol. 2, pp. 227–233). Aoyama Gakuin University.

Zampini, M. L. (1994). The role of native language transfer and task formality in the acquisition of Spanish spirantization. *Hispania, 77*(3), 470–481. https://doi.org/10.2307/344974

Zhang, J., et al. (2021). The influence of orthography on oral vocabulary acquisition in learners of Chinese as a Second Language. *Studies in Second Language Acquisition, 43*(5), 1157–1172. https://doi.org/10.1017/S0272263121000139

3 Effects of orthography on L+ phonology
A case study

The research project

The second part of this volume illustrates the methods, findings, and implications of a three-year research project that investigated — comprehensively and with a variety of methods — the effects of a single aspect of English orthography (whether a consonant is spelled with a letter or two) on all aspects of L+ phonology — perception, production, awareness, and learning — in a suitably large group of speakers of English$_{L+}$.

History of the project

During my doctoral studies in the early 2000s, I read much 1970s literature that discussed how written language affects metalinguistic awareness. For instance, scholars argued that the concepts of phoneme and word only emerge as a consequence of literacy in an alphabetic writing system, because alphabets represent sounds with letters, and words as strings of letters between spaces (for a summary of that literature and my views, see Bassetti, 2005). I realised that spelling, which affects native speakers' metalinguistic awareness, in second language speakers may affect actual pronunciation. Thus, I investigated learners of Chinese$_{L+}$ — a language I had studied as a teenager and at university — and found that the spelling of romanised Chinese affected both learners' metalinguistic awareness and their actual pronunciation (Bassetti, 2006, 2007). At that point, I noticed that I was pronouncing English consonants as geminates — long consonants — if they were spelled with double consonants, although there was no gemination in English$_{L1}$ (native) speakers' production.

The idea for the project was born, and it was simple and yet novel. The Italian language contrasts *singleton* and *geminate* (short and long) *consonants* and spells the former with a single letter and the latter with a *doublet* (double letters). English has no contrastive consonant length but has single and double consonant letter spellings. Hence, Italians may believe that an English consonant is a geminate if it is spelled with double letters, as is the case in their native Italian.

DOI: 10.4324/9780429343117-3

In 2005, I tested this hypothesis by asking ten Italian$_{L1}$-English$_{L+}$ speakers in London to listen to and then produce a series of English words. These were word pairs that contained the same voiceless stop consonants spelled with a single letter or doublet, such as the [p] in *rapidly* and *happily*. As reported in Bassetti (2008), all the participants in this pilot project produced significantly longer consonants in words written with double letters than a single letter. Clearly, I was not the only one doing this.

The beginnings of the project were not easy, as between 2005 and 2012, a conference abstract and three grant applications were all rejected. Finally, in 2012, thanks to competitive internal funds offered by the University of York, I ran some preliminary experiments. Two experiments provided proof of concept for the project and were eventually published with some modifications in Bassetti (2017); another four appeared in Bassetti and Atkinson (2015). Also in 2012, the Leverhulme Trust agreed to fund the project, with myself as Principal Investigator and Professor Jackie Masterson as the co-applicant.

The funded project ran from September 2013 to March 2017. It employed three postdoctoral Research Fellows—Drs Becky Taylor (briefly), Paolo Mairano, and Tania Cerni— and a postdoctoral Teaching Fellow— Dr Mirjana Sokolović-Perović—and was supported by four postgraduate Research Assistants—(now Drs) Emanuela Buizza, Valentina De Iacovo, Rosalba Nodari, and Alex Panicacci. There was also invaluable help from the three schools involved, in particular their English language teachers. The project, which also investigated vowel length (reported elsewhere), resulted in five journal articles (one led and first-authored by Cerni), the present volume, and fourteen conference or workshop presentations (five invited or plenary talks, seven talks, and two posters). The project also partly funded two side projects led by Mairano and Sokolović-Perović, respectively, who first authored two additional articles and six presentations.

Linguistic background

Since the project investigated consonant length in Italian$_{L1}$-English$_{L+}$ users, this section briefly introduces the consonantal inventories of the English and Italian languages before focussing on the Italian language's contrast between singleton (short) and geminate (long) consonants.

Italian and English consonants

Figure 3.1 shows the consonant systems of Standard British English and Standard Italian (respectively based on Roach, 2004, and Rogers & d'Arcangeli, 2004). From the point of view of Italian$_{L1}$ learners of English$_{L+}$, apart from differences between the inventories (five English consonants do not exist in Italian, including the notoriously difficult /θ/), two things are worth noting in

Italian

Place / Manner	Bi-labial		Labio-dental		Alveolar		Post-alveolar		Palatal		Velar	
	-	+	-	+	-	+	-	+	-	+	-	+
Nasal		m				n				ɲ		
Plosive	p	b			t	d					k	g
Trill						r						
Affricate					t͡s	d͡z	t͡ʃ	d͡ʒ				
Fricative			f	v	s	z	ʃ					
Approximant										j		w
Lateral						l				ʎ		

English

Place / Manner	Bi-labial		Labio-dental		Dental		Alveolar		Post-alveolar		Palatal		Velar		Glottal
	-	+	-	+	-	+	-	+	-	+	-	+	-	+	
Nasal		m						n						ŋ	
Plosive	p	b					t	d					k	g	
Affricate									t͡ʃ	d͡ʒ					
Fricative			f	v	θ	ð	s	z	ʃ	ʒ					h
Approximant										r		j		w	
Lateral								l							

Figure 3.1 English and Italian consonant inventories (- = voiceless; + = voiced).

the two languages: Some consonants that are transcribed and spelled similarly are phonetically different sounds; for instance, /r/ is a trill in Italian and an approximant in English; and consonant-final words are common in English but rare in Italian (Bertinetto & Loporcaro, 2005).

Consonant length in Italian

In Italian, as in various other languages (Kubozono, 2017; Ladefoged & Maddieson, 1996), there is a phonological contrast between short consonants and their long counterparts (Bertinetto & Loporcaro, 2005), also called singleton and geminate consonants respectively (Davis, 2011). A singleton and a geminate consonant can distinguish a minimal pair, such as Italian /ˈnɔte/-/ˈnɔtːe/ ('notes' and 'night', respectively, Davis, 2011). This is called 'lexical gemination' or 'true gemination', as opposed to 'syntactic' or 'false gemination', which is a longer duration caused by phonetic processes, for instance lengthening at word boundaries (Di Benedetto et al., 2021).

The main acoustic cue to a consonant length contrast is consonant duration (Kubozono, 2017; note that 'length' refers to phonology, and 'duration' to phonetics), although there are secondary cues. For instance, in Southern and Central varieties of Italian, geminate stop consonants are phonetically about twice as long as corresponding singletons (Esposito & Di Benedetto, 1999), although the geminate-singleton ratio varies across consonants (Di Benedetto et al., 2021; Di Benedetto & De Nardis, 2021). The geminate:singleton ratio is a measure of gemination, and it is calculated as the duration of the geminate divided by the duration of the corresponding singleton, so that a ratio of 1 indicates that the geminate and singleton have the same duration, whereas a ratio of 2 indicates that the geminate is twice as long as the singleton. Geminate consonants are transcribed with the consonant symbol followed by the length symbol /ː/, for instance /tː/ (elsewhere transcribed as /tt/).

In Italian, lexical gemination occurs in intervocalic position; less frequently before a glide ([aˈsːjɛme]), and for some consonants also before a lateral or trill ([ˈɔfːro], Bertinetto & Loporcaro, 2005). False gemination is also found in other positions (Payne, 2005). The present project also found that Italian speakers geminate in word-final position in loanwords (*app*, *miss*), although these geminates are shorter than those in intervocalic position (Bassetti et al., 2018). Orthographically, lexical geminates are always spelled with double letters (*doublets*), and singletons with a single consonant letter, for instance <note>-<notte> (except the 'intrinsic geminates' /ɲ ʎ ʃ t͡s d͡z/ that are always long, Payne, 2005).

Figure 3.2 shows the difference in the duration of intervocalic singleton and geminate voiceless stops produced in an Italian word reading aloud task by 30 Italian high-school students as part of this project.

In Italian, gemination is frequent, and it is important for Italians' speech processing. Geminates constitute 17% of all consonant tokens in a large corpus (Goslin et al., 2014), and the majority of consonants can geminate (/z/ cannot, and the intrinsic geminates are always long). Geminates distinguish high-frequency words (such as *casa-cassa*, 'home'-'box', in central varieties) and different morphological forms (*cadi-caddi*, 'you fall', 'I fell'). Italians perceive singleton and geminate consonants as two phonological categories with a clear boundary (Esposito & Di Benedetto, 1999), based on consonant

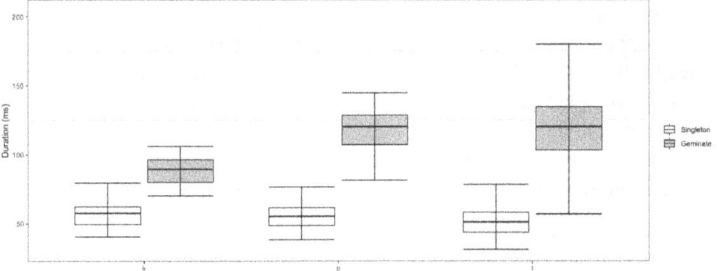

Figure 3.2 Median duration of Italian singleton and geminate voiceless stop consonants reported in Bassetti et al. (2018).

duration (Tagliapietra & McQueen, 2010). Consistent with its importance, gemination emerges in Italian infants' first words (Vihman & Majorano, 2017). Some phonologists have indeed counted singletons and geminates as different consonants, widening the consonant inventory of Italian (see Schmid, 1999).

Consonant length in English

In the English language, there is no contrastive consonant length (Davis, 2011). Longer and shorter consonants are all realisations of the same phoneme (Laver, 1994). English$_{L1}$ speakers can produce a longer consonant as a consequence of the concatenation of two morphemes that respectively end and begin with the same consonant, for instance, producing a longer [n] in *unnamed* and *fun name* than in *annoyed* (Kaye, 2005). English$_{L1}$ listeners can use this longer duration to discriminate pairs such as *topic* and *top pick* (Pickett & Decker, 1960). This is false gemination, because it has no phonological status (Oh & Redford, 2012) and consists of two rapidly articulated identical consonants rather than a long consonant (Ladefoged & Maddieson, 1996).

In written English, a consonant letter and its corresponding doublet are different spellings of the same consonant; for instance, both <t> and <tt> represent /t/. Doublets can show the quality of the preceding vowel — as in <supper> versus <super> /ˈsʌpəʳ - ˈsuːpəʳ/ — or can distinguish a proper noun from a common noun — as in *Chipp* versus *chip* (Carney, 1994). The number of consonant letters is not related to spoken consonant length, and indeed the present project demonstrated that the duration of consonants produced by English$_{L1}$ speakers is the same, regardless of their spelling (Bassetti, 2017; Bassetti et al., 2018, 2020).

Rationale and research questions

Given that English has no gemination but has consonant doublets and that in Italian doublets represent geminates, if Italians phonologically recode English$_{L+}$ words (convert them to sounds) using Italian grapheme-phoneme correspondences (GPCs), they may recode English doublets as geminates. If indeed orthographic forms affect L2 phonology, Italians would then produce and perceive geminate consonants in English words that are spelled with a consonant doublet, believe that English consonants can be singleton or geminate, and categorise consonants inside English words as singleton or geminate according to their spelling.

Previous evidence

Before this project, there was only anecdotal evidence of gemination in Italians' English speech production. An unpublished study of English pronunciation in

13 Italian primary school children reported, among other observations, that the children read [p] as 50% longer in *apple* than in other words (Browning, 2004). The researcher suggested that double consonant letters may trigger gemination, without discussing the other doublet words in the study (*yellow*, *parrot*). Just one word, in first-year primary students, in a reading aloud task, is interesting but hardly conclusive evidence.

Repetti (2006) reported no link between consonant spelling and gemination among Italian immigrants to North America who geminated word-final consonants irrespective of spelling, for instance, producing word-final geminates in both *tip* and *bill* (['tipːa], ['bilːo]). Even Canepari's (2011) book-length description of Italians' English pronunciation only mentions gemination once, presenting geminated *happy* as an example of bad pronunciation (considering '['ɛːpi]' 'less worse' than '['ɛpːpi]', p. 29). After this project began, evidence appeared that English loanwords to Italian contain intervocalic gemination caused by doublet spelling (Hamann & Colombo, 2017; Repetti, 2015), but naturalisation of foreign words is not evidence of the pronunciation of L+ speakers, as indeed loanwords can be imported without any knowledge of their phonological forms in the source language.

The second language acquisition literature consistently showed that learning consonant length contrasts in an L+ is difficult, and researchers discussed the difficulties of learners of Italian$_{L+}$ learners (De Clercq et al., 2014; Sorianello, 2014), but there was no research on the reverse situation, of learners of an L+ with no length contrasts who have a length contrast in the L1.

Research questions

Table 3.1 lists the project's research questions, arranged by aspect of L+ phonology being investigated, and followed by reference(s) to the publication(s) that addressed each question. Note that the table follows the logical order of the questions, not the chronological order of the publications. Note also that this volume only reports research on consonant length, although the project also investigated vowel length; findings related to vowels were briefly presented under Substitution earlier.

Theoretical background: Linguistic relativism and multi-competence

The project was grounded in two approaches to the study of language and language users that have long been on my mind: Multi-competence and linguistic relativism.

Linguistic relativism, or relativity, posits that our language affects the way we think (Whorf, 1956). Because different languages represent reality differently, speakers of different languages can think differently about the

Table 3.1 Research Questions and related publications.

Aspect of phonology	Research Question	Publication(s)
Production	Q1. Do Italian$_{L1}$ speakers produce singleton and geminate consonants in English$_{L+}$, depending on consonant spelling?	Bassetti (2017); Bassetti et al. (2020)
	Q2. Is Italian$_{L1}$ speakers' English$_{L+}$ gemination lexically contrastive?	Bassetti et al. (2018)
	Q3. Are there predictors of gemination in Italian$_{L1}$ speakers' English$_{L+}$ speech production?	Bassetti et al. (2020); present volume
Awareness	Q4. Do Italian$_{L1}$ speakers categorise the same English$_{L+}$ consonant as singleton versus geminate, depending on its spelling?	Bassetti et al. (2020)
Perception	Q5. Do Italian$_{L1}$ speakers perceive the same English$_{L+}$ consonant as singleton or geminate, depending on its spelling?	Bassetti et al. (2021)
All	Q6. Is there a correlation between perception, production, and categorisation of geminates in English$_{L+}$?	Present volume
Learning	Q7. Lexical learning: Do Italian$_{L1}$ speakers learn new spoken English words as containing a geminate if they learn it with a double-letters spelling?	Cerni et al. (2019)
	Q8. Phonological learning: Does learning that English has no contrastive consonant length reduce Italians' production and categorisation of geminates?	Bassetti et al. (2022)

same entities and events, reflecting the differences between their languages (for evidence, see Casasanto, 2016). Speakers of different languages often divide the same continuum into different categories, for instance, dividing the colour spectrum into different colour categories so that the English-language category 'blue' corresponds to two colour categories (roughly, dark-blue and light-blue) in languages including Greek and Russian (Boroditsky, 2003). An aspect of thought that is most clearly affected by language is the categorisation of speech sounds; for instance, sounds that English natives categorise as either /l/ or /r/ belong to the same phonological category for Japanese natives. Furthermore, not only spoken but also written language can affect thought, including thinking about language (see Cook & Bassetti, 2005); for instance, those literate in different languages may have different concepts of words (Bassetti, 2005).

The multi-competence approach proposed by Vivian Cook in the early 1990s posits that the mind of the L+ learner/user has a compound system containing more than one language (Cook, 2012). Bringing together multi-competence and linguistic relativism, Bassetti and Cook (2011) argued that the thinking of bilinguals may be affected by all the languages they know, and reviewed the evidence available at the time. There is now much research showing that bilinguals' conceptualisation and categorisation of objects and events differ from monolinguals' (Bassetti & Filipović, 2022). For instance, the concept of blue in advanced $Greek_{L1}$-$English_{L+}$ bilinguals is affected by the categories of both their languages and differs from both (Athanasopoulos, 2009).

Linguistic relativism and multi-competence warrant predictions for the present project. Since linguistic sound duration is a continuum, speakers of different languages divide it into different categories, similar to the colour spectrum. Italians have two phonological categories (short and long consonants) corresponding to one category in English. $Italian_{L1}$-$English_{L+}$ bilinguals can then be affected by spoken and written Italian and English and categorise English consonants differently from $English_{L1}$ speakers, resulting in a different perception and production.

Characteristics of the project

The research project was intended as an example of good practice in research on the effects of orthography on L+ phonology, because it addressed a number of limitations of previous studies in the field. The project was innovative in its approach, as it was a systematic investigation of the effects of a single orthographic phenomenon on all aspects of L+ phonology, and it was methodologically innovative, as it used a variety of methods and materials, some of which were purposely created for the project.

Innovative approach. The project's approach was to focus on a single phenomenon at the orthography-phonology interface — consonant substitutions caused by double letter spellings — and to investigate its effects systematically across all aspects of L+ phonology — speech production, speech perception, metalinguistic awareness, and the learning of sounds and spoken words. There was a need for research bringing together all aspects of L+ phonology, because the majority of previous studies had addressed a single OE on L+ perception, production, or learning. There was also a need to include metalinguistic awareness, which was understudied. This approach permitted us to address more ambitious research questions than previous smaller-scale studies and to test a coherent framework, so that a stronger contribution could be made to theory and methodology.

There was also a need at that stage for research on experienced L+ learners and speakers, vis-à-vis the huge amounts of research on L0s; hence, this project investigated experienced L+ learners and users with many years' experience of learning and using the L+, testing exclusively real words that were known to them (some pseudowords were needed to investigate word learning). Research on L0s is very important theoretically, to clarify underlying mechanisms of processing in the early stages of exposure to a language, and methodologically, as it allows researchers to control and manipulate variables in ways that are not possible with the limited sound repertoires and lexicons of real languages. However, it is unclear whether L0 processing reflects processing in actual language learners or users. Such OEs may occur simply because experiment participants consciously or unconsciously rely on L1 phonology and orthography to make sense of phonological input in a language they have never encountered before.

Finally, most OE studies are small-scale and only investigate small samples, whereas this study invested ample resources in the study of just one orthography-phonology correspondence in a large number of participants, using various tasks and words, and measuring many variables. All these methods required a variety of skills; therefore, the team included an applied linguist with expertise in L+ learning and use (the present author), a phonetician in charge of acoustic analysis (Mairano), a cognitive scientist in charge of statistical analysis (Cerni), and a psychologist with expertise in reading and standardised tests (Masterson).

To summarise, the project aimed at producing a much more complete picture of OEs than was the case in previous, less well-resourced projects, and had sufficient power for more complex designs and larger sets of variables.

Innovative methods. The project used a variety of tasks and materials, including specially designed ones. Methods consisted mostly of experiments, but these were corroborated by non-experimental data, crucially including qualitative data. The project was also the first to investigate the effects of a teaching intervention on OEs in L+ learners.

New tasks and sets of stimuli were needed because the project was the first experimental investigation of an orthography-induced phonological contrast that does not exist in the phonological repertoire of the target language. A new perception task had to be invented because existing tasks, which were created to investigate the perception of existing phonological contrasts, were not suitable to investigate the perception of an unattested contrast. New word lists also had to be created in order to investigate gemination in the perception and production of minimal pairs, because there was no list of homophonous word pairs differing only in the number of letters used to spell consonants (such as *finish-Finnish*).

The project demonstrated that qualitative data should play an important role in explaining experimental results in OE research. By asking participants open-ended questions, researchers can allow language users to explain in their own words what they think about the L+ phonology. While no previous OE study had collected qualitative data, such data can confirm and explain experimental results by providing insights on participants' concepts of L+ sounds and strategies used to complete tasks.

Finally, the study was the first — and as of today still the only — investigation of the effects of a teaching intervention on OEs in L+ learners. Two studies have recently looked at interventions for L0 learners (Hayes-Harb et al., 2018; Stoehr & Martin, 2022), but it is not at all clear that what works during a brief first exposure to a language has any bearing on what may work in actual language learning. Evidence from intervention studies is crucial if researchers want to establish whether OEs are at least partly reversible. This issue is not only crucial for theory, it also has practical implications for language learning and teaching.

Methods

The project used a variety of methods: Specially designed experiments to test the effects of the number of letters on consonant perception, production, awareness, and learning; qualitative data to explore meaning; standardised tests, ad hoc tasks, and questionnaires to measure individual-level variables.

Descriptions of participants, materials, tasks, and procedures in this book provide the information necessary to understand the studies. Full descriptions can be found in the individual articles.

Participants

Over 400 participants were tested. There were 260 participants in the main study, of whom 80 British English native speakers, 80 Italian$_{L1}$-English$_{L+}$ sequential bilinguals and 100 Italian$_{L1}$ learners of English$_{L+}$. These participants are described here (and in more detail in Bassetti et al., 2020). An additional 30 natives and 90 learners were tested in the pilot study (Bassetti, 2017) and 48 learners in Cerni et al. (2019); these are described in the relevant articles.

Bilinguals were native speakers of central or southern varieties of Standard Italian, who studied English as a school subject in Italy and moved to England after age 18. The learners were fourth-year high-school students recruited from three state-run non-vocational schools in Rome. In these schools, English language and literature is a compulsory school subject for three hours a week, and textbooks and related audio and video materials are in British English. Learners had received little or no naturalistic exposure: 60% had never been in an English-speaking country; the others had been on average less than 1.5 months. The median length of study with a native teacher was eight months, but with huge variation, as one-third had never had a native teacher.

As Table 3.2 shows, the learners had started learning English at a younger age compared with bilinguals, due to changes in the Italian school system. Learners also had lower levels of English proficiency and a lower frequency of use than the bilinguals. Participants reported normal or corrected-to-normal vision and no reading or listening difficulties.

Sequence of events

Learner data were collected in Italian schools during the school year 2015–2016 (October 2015–June 2016). Data from natives and bilinguals were collected in England in 2014–2016. Figure 3.3 shows the sequence of events for learners. Each learner was tested individually in three sessions, two before and one after the intervention. Sessions lasted 50 minutes, in order to fit

Table 3.2 Participants in the main study.

Descriptor	Bilinguals	Learners
Age in years (M, 95% CI)	34.19 [32.65;35.72]	16.91 *** [16.82;17.00]
English language study		
Age of onset of acquisition (years, M, 95% CI)	9.30 [8.79;9.82]	5.78 *** [5.41;6.15]
Length of English study in school (years, M, 95% CI)	8.52 [7.89;9.16]	10.50 *** [10.09;10.92]
English language proficiency (CEFR, %)		
A1/2 (beginner)	1%	31%
B1/2 (intermediate)	16%	56%
C1/2 (advanced)	83%	13%
English language use (hours per week, M, 95% CI)		
Listening	17.83 [13.88;21.78]	8.11 *** [6.19;10.02]
Reading	19.65 [15.41;23.89]	2.92 *** [1.96;3.88]
Spoken interaction	33.16 [27.37;38.95]	1.71 *** [1.05;2.37]
Native-like pronunciation importance (7=extremely important)	4.93 [4.69;5.18]	5.70 *** [5.51;5.90]
Memory (CTOPP-2 digit and pseudoword recall tasks; Wagner et al., 2013)	97.08 [94.29;99.87]	98.21 [95.76;100.67]
Self-reported imitation skills (5-point scale)	3.63 [3.21;4.05]	3.99 [3.76;4.22]

Note: *** = the two groups differed with $p < 0.001$.

Effects of orthography on L+ phonology: A case study

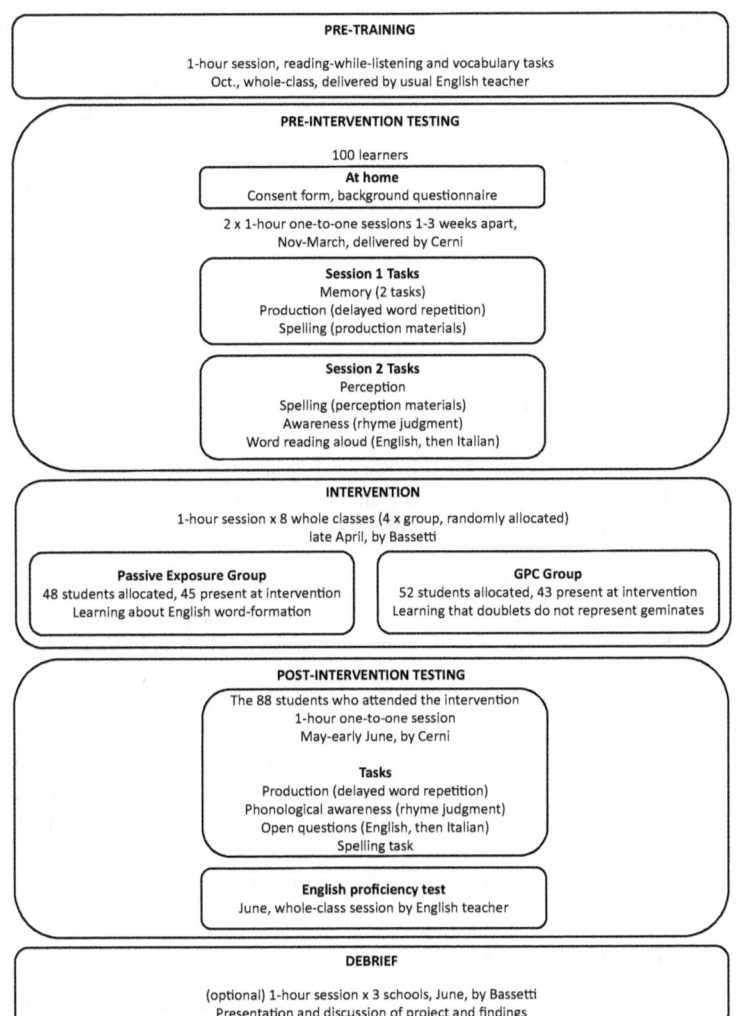

Figure 3.3 Sequence of events for learners.

within one class during normal schooling hours (sessions also included vowel data collection, not reported in this volume; see Bassetti et al., 2020). Three activities involved whole classes where participants were enrolled (including non-participants): The pre-training session, which was used to ensure that participants had been exposed to target words; the English proficiency test, whose results were given to all students as a reward for their class' participation; and the teaching interventions. Experimental tasks and materials are described in the relevant sections of Chapter 5.

Each native and bilingual was tested in one session. Bilinguals' sessions lasted two hours, with the following sequence: Perception task, perception materials spelling task, production task, production materials spelling task, awareness task, awareness open questions, memory tasks, word reading aloud task (followed by consent form, English proficiency self-rating, and questionnaire if not completed beforehand). Natives' sessions followed the same sequence as bilinguals, excluding Italian-language tasks and measures of OE predictors (memory and proficiency).

Materials

Experimental materials consisted of specially prepared word lists, plus related sets of audio recordings of female native speakers of Southern British English, and colour drawings (selected from the Art Explosion library, Nova Development, 2004). To facilitate the understanding and replication of experiments, materials are publicly available in one or both of these online repositories:

- OSF (Open Science Framework): A multidisciplinary repository provided by the charity-funded US-based Centre for Open Science (www.osf.io)
- IRIS: A specialised repository for materials used in published second language research that is UK-based and funded by the British Academy (www.iris-database.org).

Non-experimental materials included a specially prepared paper questionnaire used to collect demographic and linguistic information; an English proficiency test suitable for learners (Allan, 1992); and the CEFR descriptors (Common European Framework of Reference, Council of Europe, 2001) used to collect self-ratings of English-language proficiency from bilinguals.

Procedures and equipment

Learners' recruitment is described in detail within the description of the intervention (Question 8) in Chapter 5. Natives and bilinguals were recruited through social media and personal contacts.

Participants were tested individually in a sound-attenuated room or a quiet room in the presence of an Italian$_{L1}$-English$_{L+}$ researcher, who provided instructions and feedback on practice trials (Dr Cerni in Italy, Dr Panicacci in England; the present author tested participants in Bassetti, 2017). Researchers interacted in English with English$_{L1}$ participants and in Italian with students, while bilinguals chose the language of interaction.

Participants sat in front of a desk with an Apple laptop computer and interacted with it using a mouse (production tasks), keyboard (spelling tasks), and an IoLab response box (perception task). Experimental tasks were run in PsyScope X software (Cohen et al., 1993; Cerni et al., 2019, instead used OpenSesame 3.1.9, Mathôt et al., 2012). The experimental software managed stimulus presentation and randomisation, and recorded keyboard and mouse responses. Participants' spoken production was recorded using a digital recorder connected to a dynamic microphone.

Various measures were taken to ensure that participants and researchers performing the analyses were blinded. Participants were only informed that the study investigated English language learning, not that it focussed on pronunciation. Teachers were informed that the study investigated pronunciation but not of the nature or purposes of the intervention or the allocation of their classes to the teaching intervention or control intervention. Researchers who performed statistical and phonetic analysis ignored students' allocation.

Ethical considerations

Participation was voluntary, and consent was obtained from all participants before data collection, including parental consent for students aged 16 to 18. Participation was rewarded with cash for adults and — following parental requests — book vouchers for students. The project received ethical approval by the relevant ethics committee at the present author's employing institution.

Acoustic analysis

Consonant duration was measured following standard procedures (Turk et al., 2006) using the Praat software (Boersma & Weenink, 2016). For voiceless stop consonants, duration was measured as the duration of the closure, which is the main phonetic cue to their gemination in Italian (Pickett et al., 1999; for the measurements of the other consonants, see details in Bassetti et al., 2018). Acoustic analysis was performed by trained phoneticians: The Research Fellow, Dr Paolo Mairano, and a team trained and managed by him (Drs Buizza, De Iacovo, and Nodari; half of the data for Bassetti, 2017, and Bassetti et al., 2018, were analysed by Drs Atkinson and Sokolović-Perović, respectively). For each study, inter-rater agreement was calculated on a selection of data, and intraclass correlation coefficients ranged from 0.91 to 0.98 (all $p < 0.001$).

Statistical analysis

Data produced by previous studies have been reanalysed for this book where necessary to facilitate comparisons across studies and to reflect developments in statistical analysis in the field, as follows: Descriptive statistics report geometric instead of arithmetic means for data that were log-transformed and 95% confidence intervals instead of standard deviations. Inferential statistics consist of mixed models, which replace the ANOVAs used in early publications. Hence, some results are slightly different from previously reported ones.

Preliminary data cleaning. All datasets were cleaned before analysis. For perception and production experiments, a word pair was eliminated from analysis if the participant had misspelt one or both of the target consonants in the related spelling task, because OEs were only expected if the participant knew the consonant spelling (indeed, Sokolović-Perović et al., 2020, showed that if a participant incorrectly spelled a doublet-consonant with a single letter, they also produced it as a singleton, and vice versa, also confirmed by Cerni et al., 2019). For production experiments, measures of consonant duration (CC:C ratios) that were beyond the 99th percentile and below the 1st percentile were considered outliers and eliminated. Finally, the data were log-transformed to address the positive skew.

Initial models. Initial models were specified using a design-driven approach and included all the fixed effects and interactions of interest and the maximal random effects structure (Barr et al., 2013). Continuous data (such as consonant duration ratios) were analysed with linear mixed models using the *lmer* function in the *lmerTest* package (Kuznetsova et al., 2017). Binary data (such as correct/incorrect responses in awareness tasks) were analysed with logit mixed models with binomial distribution using the function *glmer* in the same package. Statistical analyses were run using R software 3.5.1 (R Core Team, 2018) with RStudio 1.1.456 (RStudio Team, 2018).

Model reduction. For random components, the *rePCA* function in the *RePsychLing* package (Bates et al., 2015) was used to test for overfit. Model reduction was performed through the likelihood ratio test.

Post hoc. For significant main effects, pairwise comparisons of the estimated marginal means of each level were performed using the Tukey method.

The next two chapters present and discuss results, arranged by research question.

References

Allan, D. (1992). *Oxford placement test*. Oxford University Press.
Athanasopoulos, P. (2009). Cognitive representation of colour in bilinguals: The case of Greek blues. *Bilingualism: Language and Cognition, 12*(1), 83–95.
Barr, D. J., et al. (2013). Random effects structure for confirmatory hypothesis testing: Keep it maximal. *Journal of Memory and Language, 68*(3), 255–278. https://doi.org/10.1016/j.jml.2012.11.001
Bassetti, B. (2005). Effects of writing systems on second language awareness: Word awareness in English learners of Chinese as a Foreign Language. In V. J. Cook & B. Bassetti (Eds.), *Second language writing systems* (pp. 335–356). Multilingual Matters.
Bassetti, B. (2006). Orthographic input and phonological representations in learners of Chinese as a Foreign Language. *Written Language and Literacy, 9*(1), 95–114. https://doi.org/10.1075/wll.9.1.07bas
Bassetti, B. (2007). Effects of hanyu pinyin on pronunciation in learners of Chinese as a Foreign Language. In A. Guder, X. Jiang, & Y. Wan (Eds.), *The cognition, learning*

and teaching of Chinese characters (pp. 155–179). Beijing Language and Culture University Press.
Bassetti, B. (2008). Orthographic input and second language phonology. In T. Piske & M. Young-Scholten (Eds.), *Input matters in SLA* (pp. 191–206). Multilingual Matters.
Bassetti, B. (2017). Orthography affects second language speech: Double letters and geminate production in English. *Journal of Experimental Psychology: Learning, Memory, and Cognition, 43*(11), 1835–1842. https://doi.org/10.1037/xlm0000417
Bassetti, B., & Atkinson, N. (2015). Effects of orthographic forms on pronunciation in experienced instructed second language learners. *Applied Psycholinguistics, 36*(1), 67–91. doi:10.1017/S0142716414000435
Bassetti, B., Cerni, T., & Masterson, J. (2022). The efficacy of grapheme-phoneme correspondence instruction in reducing the effect of orthographic forms on second language phonology. *Applied Psycholinguistics, 43*(3), 683–705. DOI: 10.1017/S014271642200008X
Bassetti, B., & Cook, V. J. (2011). Language and cognition: The second language user. In V. J. Cook & B. Bassetti (Eds.), *Language and bilingual cognition* (pp. 143–190). Psychology Press.
Bassetti, B., & Filipović, L. (2022). Researching language and cognition in bilinguals. *International Journal of Bilingualism, 26*(1), 3–12. https://doi.org/10.1177/13670069211022860
Bassetti, B., Mairano, P., Masterson, J., & Cerni, T. (2020). Effects of orthographic forms on phonological awareness and speech production in second language speakers, with consideration of speaker variables. *Language Learning, 70*(4), 1218–1256. doi:10.1111/lang.12423
Bassetti, B., Masterson, J., Cerni, T., & Mairano, P. (2021). Orthographic forms affect speech perception in a second language: Consonant and vowel length in L2 English. *Journal of Experimental Psychology: Human Perception and Performance, 47*, 1583–1603. doi:10.1037/xhp0000949
Bassetti, B., Sokolović-Perović, M., Mairano, P., & Cerni, T. (2018). Orthography-induced length contrasts in the second language phonological systems of L2 speakers of English: Evidence from minimal pairs. *Language and Speech, 61*(4), 577–597. doi:10.1177/0023830918780141
Bates, D., et al. (2015). *Parsimonious mixed models*. In arXiv preprint arXiv:1506.04967.
Bertinetto, P. M., & Loporcaro, M. (2005). The sound pattern of Standard Italian, as compared with the varieties spoken in Florence, Milan and Rome. *Journal of the International Phonetic Association, 35*(2), 131–151. https://doi.org/10.1017/s0025100305002148
Boersma, P., & Weenink, D. (2016). Praat: Doing phonetics by computer (Version 6.0.19) [Computer software]. Retrieved from http://www.praat.org/
Boroditsky, L. (2003). Linguistic relativity. In L. Nadel (Ed.), *Encyclopedia of cognitive science* (Vol. 2, pp. 917–921). MacMillan Publishers.
Browning, S. R. (2004). *Analysis of Italian children's English pronunciation*. Report contributed to the EU FP5 PF STAR Project, led by Martin Russell. Retrieved June 1, 2021, from www.eee.bham.ac.uk/russellm/ItalianEnglishReport/ItalianEnglish_report_v2.htm
Canepari, L. (2011). *Pronuncia inglese per italiani*. Aracne.
Carney, E. (1994). *A survey of English spelling*. Routledge.
Casasanto, D. (2016). Linguistic relativity. In N. Riemer (Ed.), *Routledge handbook of semantics* (pp. 158–174). Routledge.

Cerni, T., Bassetti, B., & Masterson, J. (2019). Effects of orthographic forms on the acquisition of novel spoken words in a second language. *Frontiers in Communication,4*, 31. doi:10.3389/fcomm.2019.00031

Cohen, J., et al. (1993). PsyScope: An interactive graphic system for designing and controlling experiments in the psychology laboratory using Macintosh computers. *Behavior Research Methods, Instruments, & Computers, 25*(2), 257–271.

Cook, V. J. (2012). Multi-competence. In C. A. Chapelle (Ed.), *The encyclopedia of applied linguistics* (pp. 3768–3774). Wiley-Blackwell.

Cook, V. J., & Bassetti, B. (2005). An introduction to researching second language writing systems. In V. J. Cook & B. Bassetti (Eds.), *Second language writing systems* (pp. 1–67). Multilingual Matters.

Council of Europe. (2001). *Common European framework of reference for languages: Learning, teaching, assessment (CEFR)*. Council of Europe. www.coe.int/t/dg4/linguistic/cadre1_en.asp

Davis, S. (2011). Geminates. In M. van Oostendrop, C. J. Ewen, E. Hume, & K. Rice (Eds.), *The Blackwell companion to phonology* (Vol. 2. Suprasegmental and prosodic phonology, pp. 873–897). Wiley-Blackwell. https://doi.org/10.1002/9781444335262.wbctp0037

De Clercq, B., et al. (2014). Rosa versus rossa: The acquisition of Italian geminates by native speakers of Dutch. *Phrasis: Studies in Language and Literature, 2*, 3–29.

Di Benedetto, M. G., & De Nardis, L. (2021). Consonant gemination in Italian: The nasal and liquid case. *Speech Communication, 133*, 62–80.

Di Benedetto, M. G., et al. (2021). Lexical and syntactic gemination in Italian consonants—Does a geminate Italian consonant consist of a repeated or a strengthened consonant? *The Journal of the Acoustical Society of America, 149*, 3375–3386.

Esposito, A., & Di Benedetto, M. G. (1999). Acoustical and perceptual study of gemination in Italian stops. *Journal of the Acoustical Society of America, 106*(4), 2051–2062. https://doi.org/10.1121/1.428056

Goslin, J., et al. (2014). PhonItalia: A phonological lexicon for Italian. *Behavior Research Methods, 46*(3), 872–886. https://doi.org/10.3758/s13428-013-0400-8.

Hamann, S., & Colombo, I. E. (2017). A formal account of the interaction of orthography and perception. *Natural Language & Linguistic Theory, 35*(3), 683–714. https://doi.org/10.1007/s11049-017-9362-3

Hayes-Harb, R., Brown, K., & Smith, B. L. (2018). Orthographic input and the acquisition of German final devoicing by native speakers of English. *Language and Speech, 61*(4), 547–564. https://doi.org/10.1177/0023830917710048

Kaye, A. S. (2005). Gemination in English. *English Today, 21*, 43–55. https://doi.org/10.1017/S0266078405002063

Kubozono, H. (Ed.). (2017). *The phonetics and phonology of geminate consonants*. Oxford University Press.

Kuznetsova, A., et al. (2017). lmerTest: Tests in linear mixed effects models. https://CRAN.R-project.org/package=lmerTest

Ladefoged, P., & Maddieson, I. (1996). *The sounds of the world's languages*. Blackwell Publishing.

Laver, J. (1994). *Principles of phonetics*. Cambridge University Press. https://doi.org/10.1017/cbo9781139166621

Mathôt, S., et al. (2012). OpenSesame: An open-source, graphical experiment builder for the social sciences. *Behavior Research Methods, 44*(2), 314–324.

Nova Development. (2004). *Art explosion library*. Nova Development Co.

Oh, G. E., & Redford, M. A. (2012). The production and phonetic representation of fake geminates in English. *Journal of Phonetics, 40*(1), 82–91. https://doi.org/10.1016/j.wocn.2011.08.003

Payne, E. M. (2005). Phonetic variation in Italian consonant gemination. *Journal of the International Phonetic Association, 35*(2), 153–181. https://doi.org/10.1017/s0025100305002240

Pickett, E. R., et al. (1999). Effects of speaking rate on the singleton/geminate consonant contrast in Italian. *Phonetica, 56*(3–4), 135–157. https://doi.org/10.1159/000028448

Pickett, J. M., & Decker, L. R. (1960). Time factors in perception of a double consonant. *Language and Speech, 3*(1), 11–17.

R Core Team. (2018). *R: A language and environment for statistical computing.* R. Foundation for Statistical Computing. www.R-project.org

Repetti, L. (2006). The emergence of marked structures in the integration of loans in Italian. *Amsterdam Studies in the Theory and History of Linguistic Science Series 4, 274,* 209.

Repetti, L. (2015). A note on English loan words in American Italian and Standard Italian. In R. Harvey & P. Nganang (Eds.), *Realism and its vicissitudes: Essays in honor of Sandy Petrey.* Peter Lang.

Roach, P. (2004). British English: Received pronunciation. *Journal of the International Phonetic Association, 34*(21), 239–245.

Rogers, D., & d'Arcangeli, L. (2004). Italian. *Journal of the International Phonetic Association, 34*(1), 117–121.

RStudio Team. (2018). *RStudio: Integrated development for R.* Boston, MA. www.rstudio.com

Schmid, S. (1999). *Fonetica e fonologia dell'italiano contemporaneo.* Paravia.

Sokolović-Perović, M., Bassetti, B., & Dillon, S. (2020). English orthographic forms affect L2 English speech production in native users of a non-alphabetic writing system. *Bilingualism: Language and Cognition, 23*(3), 591–601. https://doi.org/10.1017/s136672891900035x

Sorianello, P. (2014). Italian geminate consonants in L2 acquisition. In L. Costamagna & C. Celata (Eds.), *Consonant gemination in first and second language acquisition* (pp. 25–46). Pacini Editore.

Stoehr, A., & Martin, C. D. (2022). Orthography affects L1 and L2 speech perception but not production in early bilinguals. *Bilingualism: Language and Cognition, 25*(1), 108–120. https://doi.org/https://doi.org/10.1017/S1366728921000523

Tagliapietra, L., & McQueen, J. M. (2010). What and where in speech recognition: Geminates and singletons in spoken Italian. *Journal of Memory and Language, 63,* 306–323. https://doi.org/10.1016/j.jml.2010.05.001

Turk, A., Nakai, S., & Sugahara, M. (2006). Acoustic segment durations in prosodic research: A practical guide. In S. Sudhoff, D. Lenertova, R. Meyer, S. Pappert, P. Augurzky, I. Mleinek, N. Richter, & J. Schließer (Eds.), *Methods in empirical prosody research* (pp. 1–28). de Gruyter. https://doi.org/10.1515/9783110914641.1

Vihman, M., & Majorano, M. (2017). The role of geminates in infants' early word production and word-form recognition. *Journal of Child Language, 44*(1), 158–184.

Wagner, R. K., Torgersen, J. K., Rashotte, C. A., & Pearson, N. A. (2013). *Comprehensive Test of Phonological Processing – Second Edition (CTOPP-2).* PsycTESTS. https://doi.org/10.1037/t52630-000

Whorf, B. L. (1956). *Language, thought and reality: Selected writings of Benjamin Lee Whorf* (J. B. Carroll, Ed.). The MIT Press.

4 Effects of orthography on L+ speech production

Question 1: Do Italian$_{L1}$ speakers produce singleton and geminate consonants in English$_{L+}$, depending on consonant spelling?

Yes. Italians produce the same English$_{L+}$ consonant as a singleton if it is spelled with a single consonant letter or as a geminate if it is spelled with a doublet, for instance producing a longer [t] in *kitty* than in *city*. The mean geminate:singleton ratio is above 1.5.

Question 1a: Do Italians produce singleton and geminate consonants in English$_{L+}$?

Bassetti (2017, Experiment 1) established for the first time the existence of gemination in English$_{L+}$. Since this was an exploratory study, it aimed at maximising the chances of detecting an OE, if there was one. For this reason, the experiment tested participants that are most likely to be affected by orthography — instructed learners — and adopted a task that is most likely to reveal OEs — a word reading aloud task.

Table 4.1 shows Experiment 1's design at a glance. The learners were Italian high-school students. English$_{L1}$ speakers were also tested to ensure that orthography does not affect consonant length in native English speech, because there was no empirical evidence of this. The Italians had been studying (mostly British) English as a school subject for over a decade (M = 11.5 years, SD = 2.8).

Participants' task was to read aloud 18 English words. The words belonged to nine word-pairs, such that within each pair the same target consonant appeared in the same phonological context (same preceding vowel, same following vowel or glide) and stress pattern, but in one word it was spelled with a letter and in the other word with a doublet (double letters). For example, in the pair *city* and *kitty* (['sɪti], ['kɪti]) the consonant [t] is spelled with a letter or doublet, respectively, and it occurs in the same post-tonic position in the intervocalic context /ɪ_i/. Thus, the voiceless stop [t] is the target consonant, *city* is a

DOI: 10.4324/9780429343117-4

'C-word' (single-consonant-letter word) that contains a 'C-consonant' (spelled with a single consonant letter), and *kitty* is a 'CC-word' (consonant-doublet word) that contains a 'CC-consonant' (spelled with consonant doublets). There were three word pairs for each of the three English voiceless stop consonants [p], [t], [k]. Voiceless stop consonants were chosen because there is general agreement on the measurement of their duration, and the characteristics of their gemination in Italian have been widely studied and are well-established.

Table 4.1 Summary of design, Experiment 1, Bassetti (2017).

Methods			Design	
Participants	Materials	Task	IV	DV
30 natives; 30 learners	9 C-CC pairs (targets: Voiceless stops, e.g., *city-kitty*)	Word reading aloud	Language background (between: Natives, learners)	CC:C ratio

Note: IV = independent variable; DV = dependent variable.

A word reading aloud task was used to maximise the potential impact of orthography, as it allows participants to focus on form (pronunciation). Words were presented in print, marked with underlining within sentences to aid recognition. Each participant produced each word orally three times within the carrier sentence *The word ___ is missing*, which puts the target word in nuclear position at the centre of the intonational unit, for instance saying *The word kitty is missing*. The three repetitions were later used to obtain a mean duration for the target consonant, which would be more stable than just one repetition.

Table 4.2 shows the study's predictions and results at a glance. Italians produced the same consonant as long when spelled with a doublet and as short when spelled with a letter, as CC-consonants were on average more than 1.5 times as long as the corresponding C-consonants. The two spectrograms in Figure 4.1 illustrate the production of *city* and *kitty* by the same

Table 4.2 Predictions and results, Experiment 1, Bassetti (2017).

Predictions	Results
1a. Learners: CC:C ratio > 1 (the same consonant is produced longer if spelled with CC than if spelled with C).	✓ mean ratio = 1.58, 95% CI [1.53;1.64]
1b. Natives: CC:C ratio = 1 (consonant duration is not affected by its spelling).	✓ mean ratio = 0.96, 95% CI [0.93;0.98])
2. CC:C ratio is higher among learners than natives.	✓ $p < 0.001$

48 Effects of orthography on L+ speech production

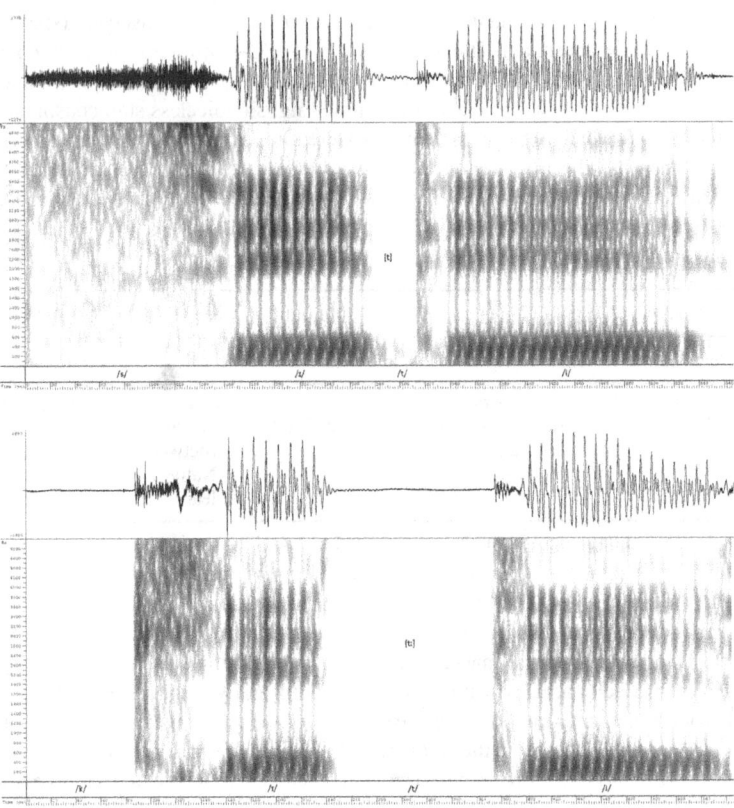

Figure 4.1 Spectrograms of [ˈsɪtɪ] and [ˈkɪtɪ] uttered by an Italian participant.

Note: The phonemic transcription at the bottom shows the target sounds.

Italian participant. English$_{L1}$ speakers produced consonants of similar duration regardless of the number of letters in their spelling, with a mean CC:C ratio very close to one. (Note that all means reported in this chapter are geometric means.)

The final model, *RATIO_LOG ~ LANGUAGE_BACKGROUND + (1|PARTICIPANT) + (1|WORD_PAIR)*, confirmed that the CC:C ratio was higher among learners than L1 speakers ($p < 0.001$).

This experiment provided the first ever evidence of a possible phonological contrast between singleton consonants and geminate consonants in English$_{L+}$. This was also the first evidence that native English speakers do not produce consonants of different duration in relation to spelling.

However, this effect of spelling on consonant production during reading aloud may be caused by the presence of orthographic input. The next experiment tested whether Italians produce orthography-induced geminates in the absence of orthographic input and, if so, whether such OE is stronger with than without orthographic input.

Question 1b: Do Italians produce orthography-induced gemination in the absence of orthographic input? And if so, is the effect weaker than in the presence of orthographic input?

The second experiment reported in Bassetti (2017) found that Italians produce geminates in spoken English$_{L+}$ words not only when reading aloud but also when there is no orthographic input. Students from the same school as those in Experiment 1 produced the same 18 words, but the task consisted of repeating spoken words. To further clarify the role of orthographic input, half of the participants received only auditory input (AI group); the other half received both auditory and orthographic input simultaneously (AOI group). Table 4.3 shows the design.

As Figure 4.2 shows, the sequence of events consisted of two parts: Phrase learning, and target word production. There were five steps, two of which differed across the two groups:

1. See a picture, then listen to a recorded native speaker's production of a six-word phrase related to the picture (the picture helps understand the phrase)
2. Count backwards from seven to one (counting removes traces of the native's production from phonological memory)
3. Repeat the phrase (repeating shows whether the participant remembers the phrase. If not, they can repeat steps 1–3 up to three times)
4. Listen to a truncated version of the same phrase, from which the target word and all that followed were eliminated.

Table 4.3 Summary of design, Experiment 2, Bassetti (2017).

Methods			Design	
Participants	Materials	Task	IV	DV
Two groups of 30 learners: Auditory Input (AI) and Auditory-Orthographic Input (AOI)	9 C-CC pairs (same as Experiment 1)	Delayed word repetition	Type of Input (between: AI, AOI)	CC:C ratio

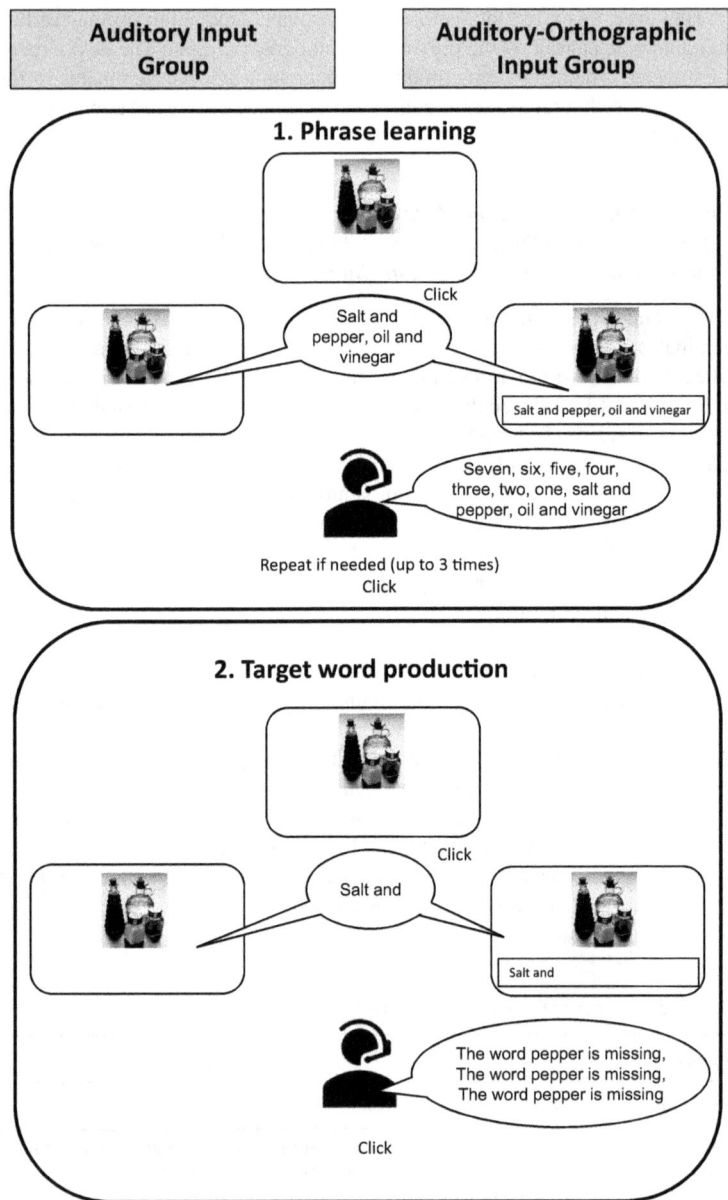

Figure 4.2 Schematic representation of the Delayed Word Repetition Task.

Notes: This is a schematic diagram, that is to say, simplified and not to scale. Photograph source: www.123rf.com.

5 Repeat the first missing word (the target word) in a carrier sentence three times (the carrier sentence puts the target word in nuclear position in the intonational unit).

The Auditory-Orthographic Input group also saw the spelling of the complete phrase at step 1 and of the truncated phrase at step 4. Spelling appeared simultaneously with the onset of the audio recording and disappeared simultaneously with its end.

Table 4.4 summarises the results. The same consonant was produced on average 1.6 times as long when spelled with a doublet than when spelled with a letter. The final model, *RATIO_LOG ~ (1|PARTICIPANT) + (1|WORD_PAIR)*, revealed that the effect of consonant spelling on the CC:C ratio was very similar in the two groups, regardless of whether they had seen orthographic input or not. Results show that Italian$_{L1}$ speakers produce geminate and singleton consonants in English$_{L+}$ even when repeating what they just heard from an English$_{L1}$ speaker without orthographic input. However, this experiment was only a small-case study with few participants and words. This question is worth investigating again, as previous studies linked the presence of orthographic input to stronger OEs (Bassetti & Atkinson, 2015; Shea, 2017). In conclusion, this first study provided proof of concept for the larger-scale study to follow, described in the next section.

Question 1c: Does naturalistic exposure eliminate or reduce orthography-induced gemination in production?

The main study's production task (Experiment 1, Bassetti et al., 2020) tested whether lengthy naturalistic exposure can eliminate or reduce OEs on L+ speech production by comparing instructed learners and sequential bilinguals with lengthy residence in an English-speaking environment.

This experiment was much larger than the previous two: 260 participants produced a total of 25,200 token words. This large sample allowed for a

Table 4.4 Predictions and results, Experiment 2, Bassetti (2017).

Predictions	Results
1. Both groups: CC:C ratio > 1 (the same consonant is produced as longer if spelled with CC than if spelled with C).	✓ Across groups, mean ratio = 1.60, 95% CI [1.55;1.64]
2. CC:C ratio is higher (i.e., stronger OEs) in the Auditory-Orthographic Input group than in the Auditory Input group	✓ No group differences. AOI group ratio = 1.61 [1.55;1.67] AI group ratio = 1.58 [1.52;1.65]

meaningful exploration of variables that may predict OEs on L2 speech production (see Question 3).

Table 4.5 shows the design. There were three groups: English$_{L1}$ speakers, Italian$_{L1}$-English$_{L+}$ bilinguals, and Italian$_{L1}$ learners of English$_{L+}$. The prediction was that consonant spelling should affect all L+ speakers but should affect learners more than bilinguals, because bilinguals had been living in an English-speaking environment for over six years on average, whereas the learners had only studied English as a school subject (see Participants in Chapter 3).

The 20 word pairs contained a target voiceless stop and included the nine pairs used in Bassetti (2017). The task was the same Delayed Word Repetition task employed in Experiment 2 in that article (without orthographic input), but with different pictures and a different carrier sentence. Since the task was too time-consuming for learners, each learner produced 20 words (10 pairs), randomly presented from one of two counterbalanced lists. OEs were only predicted if the participant knew whether the target consonant was spelled with one or two letters; therefore, two measures were taken to ensure that participants knew the target spelling. First, learners were exposed to each word once in the teaching session that ran at the beginning of the project (see Figure 4.3). Second,

Table 4.5 Summary of design, Experiment 1, Bassetti et al. (2020).

Methods			Design	
Participants	Materials	Task	IV	DV
80 natives, 80 bilinguals, and 100 learners	20 C-CC pairs (voiceless stops)	Delayed word repetition (then spelling)	Language background (between: Natives, bilinguals, learners)	CC:C ratio

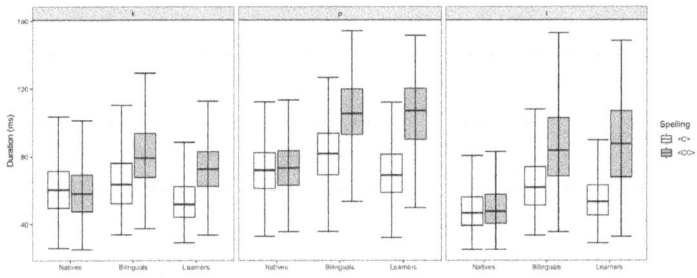

Figure 4.3 Singleton and geminate durations across the three production experiments.

Table 4.6 Predictions and results, Experiment 1, Bassetti et al. (2020).

Predictions	Results
1.a Both L+ groups (learners, bilinguals): CC:C ratio > 1.	✓ Mean ratios: Bilinguals = 1.33 [1.31, 1.35] Learners = 1.53 [1.50, 1.56]
1.b Natives: Ratio = 1	✓ Natives: 1.01 [1.00, 1.02]
1.c Ratio higher in L+ speakers than natives	✓ Bilinguals-natives: $p < 0.001$ Learners-natives: $p < 0.001$
2. Ratio higher in learners than bilinguals	✓ $p < 0.001$

after the production task, a Word Spelling Task was used to check that participants knew the number of letters in the spelling of each word. For each word, participants were shown the relevant picture and the written sentence with a gap replacing the target word. After hearing a recording of the sentence, they typed the missing word. Words that had been misspelt were not entered in the acoustic analysis.

As Table 4.6 shows, the mean CC:C ratio was just above 1.5 in learners, around 1.3 in bilinguals, and around one in natives. The final model, *RATIO_LOG ~ LANGUAGE_BACKGROUND + (1|PARTICIPANT) + (1|WORD_PAIR)*, and post-hoc tests showed that the ratio was higher among learners than bilinguals, revealing that bilinguals' long naturalistic exposure and/or higher proficiency may reduce the magnitude of OEs on speech production. The ratio was also higher among L+ speakers than L1 speakers, confirming that consonant duration in English$_{L1}$ speech production is unrelated to spelling, whereas Italian$_{L1}$ speakers of English$_{L+}$ produce orthography-induced geminates.

Bringing it all together: Geminate and singleton durations and geminate:singleton ratios across experiments

To fully understand the results of the speech production studies reported above, the next step was to bring together all the data. A dataset was then created with all the valid intervocalic voiceless stop consonants produced across the three experiments reported earlier. Figure 4.3 shows the mean durations of geminates and singletons, by group and by consonant.

Figure 4.3 shows that Italians' English$_{L+}$ singleton and geminates are two different phonological categories, as there is no overlap in the durations of singleton and geminate consonants produced by either bilinguals or learners. The figure also shows that singletons and geminates differed more among learners than among bilinguals. Finally, there was high inter-individual variability.

The analysis of the whole dataset also confirmed that CC:C ratios are higher in learners than bilinguals ($p < 0.001$). The geminate:singleton ratios were (geometric means, 95% CIs):

Natives: 1.00 [0.99;1.01]
Bilinguals: 1.33 [1.31;1.35]
Learners: 1.55 [1.52;1.57]

To summarise, the three experiments reported earlier showed that Italians produce English consonants as singletons or geminates, corresponding to single letter or doublet spelling. The next experiment moved one step further by testing whether Italians use the singleton-geminate contrast to distinguish minimal pairs.

Question 2: Is Italian$_{L1}$ speakers' English$_{L+}$ gemination lexically contrastive?

Yes. Italians produce singleton or geminate consonants to distinguish English homophones that are spelled with a letter or doublet, for instance producing the orthographic minimal pair *finish-Finnish* (both [ˈfɪnɪʃ]) as a phonological minimal pair distinguished by a singleton [n] in *finish* and a geminate [nː] in *Finnish*.

The next experiment (Bassetti et al., 2018) investigated whether Italians use singleton and geminate consonants to distinguish English words in their speech production. This was a crucial question because in phonology the existence of minimal pairs is evidence that a phonetic difference is a phonological contrast.

As Table 4.7 shows, materials were pairs of English homophonic words containing the same target consonant spelled with a letter or doublet, such

Table 4.7 Summary of design, Bassetti et al. (2018).

Methods			Design		
Participants	Materials	Task	IV		DV
Natives, bilinguals, and learners (30 each)	19 C-CC homophonic word pairs (e.g., *finish-Finnish*)	Word reading aloud	Language background (between: Natives, bilinguals, learners)		CC:C ratio

as *finish* and *Finnish* (both [ˈfɪnɪʃ]). To English$_{L1}$ speakers, the pair of homophones *finish-Finnish* is an orthographic minimal pair, distinguished by two different spellings of the same consonant. If Italians contrast singleton and geminate consonants in English$_{L+}$, and if gemination is caused by the consonant's orthographic form (doublet), they should produce *finish-Finnish* as a phonological minimal pair, namely [ˈfɪnɪʃ]-[ˈfɪnːɪʃ], distinguished by two different phonemes (*finish* with a singleton [n] and *Finnish* with a geminate [nː]). This would be in line with Italian *cane-canne* ('dog-reeds'), which is both an orthographic minimal pair and a phonological minimal pair [ˈkane]-[ˈkanːe].

As in Bassetti et al. (2020), the experiment compared instructed learners and sequential bilinguals to test whether naturalistic exposure reduces gemination. English$_{L1}$ speakers were also included to show that they do not use consonant duration to disambiguate homophones. The word reading aloud task was similar to Experiment 1 in Bassetti (2017). Participants received a printed list of phrases, each with an underlined word, such as *Mr Sven Hjerson, the famous Finnish detective*, and produced the underlined word within a carrier sentence three times. However, there were more target words than in the earlier study, for two reasons. First, to test for effects of L1 phonotactics, eight CC-consonants were in a position where gemination is illegal — that is to say, not attested — in native Italian words but is found in loanwords, acronyms, and similar, namely in word-final position (*add*) or in a syllable-final consonant cluster (*missed*, [mɪst]). If L1 phonotactics moderate OEs, gemination should be rarer or absent in English words where its position would be illegal in Italian. Second, a variety of target consonants were included, not just voiceless stops. This was meant to better represent the variety of the English lexicon and consonant inventory. It was also necessary because there are not many homophonic pairs that contain the same consonant spelled with a single letter or doublet and are familiar enough to high-school students. Because of the limited number of suitable homophonic pairs, some pairs had spelling differences other than the spelling of the target consonant, such as the different vowel spelling in *bury-berry*.

The spectrograms in Figure 4.4 show the different durations of [n] in the words *finish* and *Finnish* uttered by the same learner. Table 4.8 summarises the results of the experiment.

The final model *RATIO_LOG ~ LANGUAGE_BACKGROUND + (1|PARTICIPANT) + (1|WORD_PAIR)* and post-hoc tests confirmed that English$_{L1}$ speakers pronounced CC- and C-consonants with similar duration, and L+ speakers produced CC-consonants as longer than C-consonants. However, there were no differences between bilinguals and learners. In light of the results of the whole project, these null results are best explained as a consequence of the small sample size.

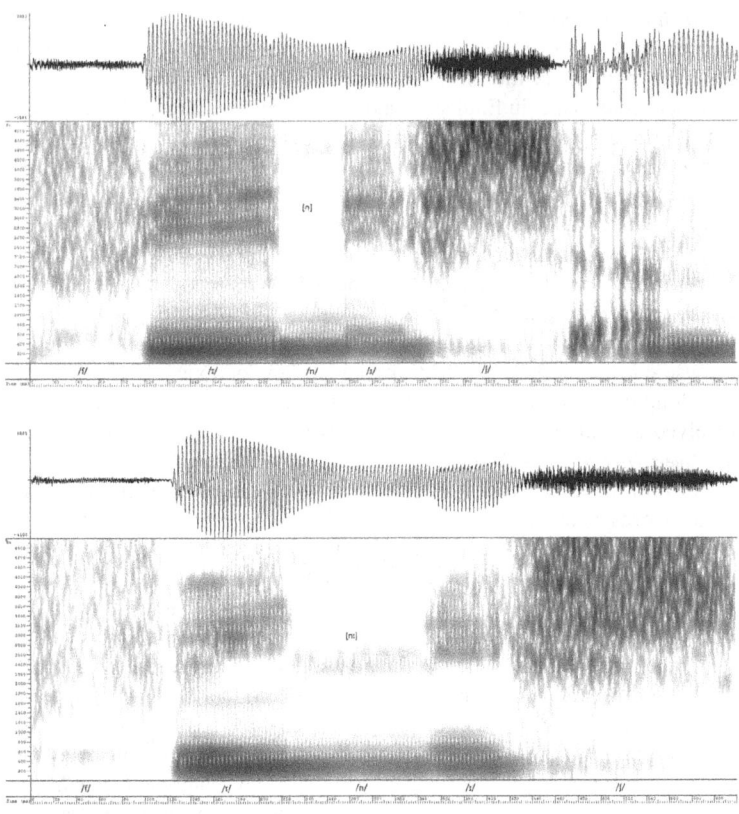

Figure 4.4 Spectrograms of *finish* and *Finnish* uttered by a learner.

Note: The phonemic transcription at the bottom shows the target sounds.

Table 4.8 Predictions and results, Bassetti et al. (2018).

Predictions	Results
1.a L+ speakers: CC:C ratio > 1 (homophones produced as a phonological minimal pair distinguished by a singleton [C] or geminate [C:])	✓ Bilinguals' overall ratio = 1.20 [1.17;1.23] - intervocalic: 1.29 [1.25;1.33] - Italian-illegal: 1.08 [1.04;1.12] - learners' overall ratio = 1.20 [1.17;1.24] - intervocalic: 1.29 [1.25;1.34] - Italian-illegal: 1.10 [1.06;1.14]
1.b Natives: Ratio = 1	✓ Natives: 1.03 [1.01, 1.04] - intervocalic: 1.04 [1.00;1.07] - Italian-illegal: 1.02 [1.00;1.04]
1.c Ratio higher (stronger effects) in L+ speakers than natives.	✓ Bilinguals-natives: $p < 0.001$ Learners-natives: $p < 0.001$
2. Ratio higher in learners than bilinguals	✗ $p = 0.986$

Effects of orthography on L+ speech production 57

In conclusion, results confirmed that consonant length is contrastive in the English$_{L+}$ phonological system of Italian$_{L1}$ speakers, who therefore produce English orthographic minimal pairs as phonological minimal pairs distinguished by the gemination of one consonant (the one spelled with a doublet). This phonological contrast is not attested in L+ speakers' production.

The next issue was explaining the huge levels of variability found in all experiments. All datasets presented so far revealed much inter-individual variability (see Figure 4.3), and indeed all models contained by-participant and by-item intercepts as random effects. The next issue was to identify some variables that may explain this variability.

Question 3: Are there predictors of geminate production in Italians' English$_{L+}$ production?

Yes. Looking at individual-level predictors, stronger OEs on English$_{L+}$ speech production (higher CC:C ratio) were predicted by lower proficiency in both learners and bilinguals, and by weaker short-term memory in bilinguals only. Looking at item-level (word/sound) predictors, the ratio was influenced by L1 phonotactics (higher in intervocalic position) and type of consonant (highest with [t]), whereas the impact of L1 cognates was unclear.

Having established that Italians produce orthography-induced geminates in English$_{L+}$, the next question was: Are there variables that modulate the magnitude of such effects, that is to say, are linked to higher or lower levels of gemination in speech production? It was the main aim of this project to investigate which (if any) characteristics of L+ speakers, words, or sounds could result in stronger OEs on production, a question that could not be answered by smaller-scale studies. This first systematic investigation of the impact of characteristics of the L+ speaker found that higher levels of gemination were associated with lower L+ proficiency, and for bilinguals only with weaker short-term memory. The CC:C ratio was also higher in intervocalic positions than positions where gemination is illegal in the L1, and varied across types of consonants, with [t] showing the highest ratio. It was unclear whether L1 cognates have an impact. In general, more research is needed before conclusions can be drawn.

Individual-level predictors of English$_{L+}$ gemination

Bassetti et al. (2020) measured a number of individual-level variables, that is to say, characteristics of the L+ speaker, including some that had been previously shown to affect L+ pronunciation, such as the ability to mimic linguistic sounds, and others that may be expected to impact OEs specifically, such as the relative amount of exposure to written versus spoken input. Data were collected by means of standardised tests and a questionnaire (fully described in Bassetti et al., 2020, and available in the OSF repository). The variables were:

- Cognitive individual differences:
  - short-term memory
  - phonological aptitude: mimicry ability (ability to imitate dialects and foreign accents).
- $English_{L+}$ learning:
  - age of onset of acquisition
  - length of instruction
  - proficiency.
- $English_{L+}$ exposure and use:
  - amount of interaction in English
  - length of residence in an English-speaking country
  - proportion of written input out of total (written and spoken) input
  - learners: length of study with native-speaking teachers
  - bilinguals: proportion of English use out of total (English and Italian) language use.
- Motivation and attitudes:
  - perceived importance of a native-like pronunciation
  - desire for native-like pronunciation
  - learners: motivation for learning English
  - learners: attitudes towards English pronunciation (Pronunciation Attitude Inventory)
  - bilinguals: integrative motivation (desire to integrate in the British society)
  - bilinguals: attitudes towards English (L2 emotionality).
- Pronunciation learning (learners only):
  - pronunciation learning strategies.

Two separate regression analyses were run for learners and bilinguals, for both practical and theoretical reasons. First, there were intrinsic differences between the two groups that would constitute confounding variables and produce spurious findings. For instance, the age of onset of acquisition was higher in bilinguals than in learners. Second, predictors of OEs are likely to differ between instructed learners and naturalistic users; for instance, phonological aptitude may help naturalistic users who are immersed in a native input-rich environment more than learners in a classroom.

Lower English$_{L+}$ proficiency predicted stronger OEs on production (higher geminate:singleton ratio) in both learners ($p = .003$) and bilinguals ($p = .006$). This extends some previous evidence that proficiency is linked to pronunciation (e.g., Iwashita et al., 2008) to OEs. Among bilinguals only, stronger short-term memory also predicted weaker OEs *(p = .030)*. Perhaps better spoken input processing is important in an input-rich environment but less so in a classroom, where spoken input is limited and may be non-targetlike. The other variables did not appear to predict OEs.

While all the variables mentioned earlier were tested within each group, the effects of naturalistic exposure were tested by comparing learners and bilinguals. Bassetti et al. (2020) reported higher levels of gemination among learners than sequential bilinguals. These results contradicted null results reported in previous publications by the same researchers (Bassetti et al., 2018; Mairano et al., 2018), which were probably due to a lack of power, as these earlier studies tested smaller sub-samples of the group of main study participants. In spite of statistical significance, differences were not huge, and the studies of perception and awareness reported in the next chapter found no such differences. Lengthy naturalistic exposure seems unlikely to reduce orthography-induced gemination, although this remains open to investigation. Importantly, it does not eliminate gemination.

Other predictors of English$_{L+}$ gemination

To test whether orthography-induced gemination may be influenced by item-level — that is to say, sound-level or word-level — variables, a number of variables were measured, including variables related to L1 gemination and variables related to orthographic forms.

Variables related to L1 gemination. Gemination was found in positions where it is not attested in Italian native words — word-final (*add*) or in syllable coda (*missed*) — but the CC:C ratio was lower than in intervocalic positions (learners: $p = 0.002$; bilinguals: $p < .001$; data from Bassetti et al., 2018, re-analysed for the present publication). The impact of L1 cognates and loanwords is unclear. Bassetti et al. (2018, 2020) found slightly stronger effects in English words that had an Italian loanword or cognate containing a doublet, such as English *roll* (Italian *rollare*), but no weaker effects in words whose Italian cognate contained a singleton, such as *carrot* (Italian *carota*).

However, Bassetti (2017) and a reanalysis of the whole dataset found no impact of Italian cognates and loanwords.

Variables related to items (words and consonants). A number of item-level variables were measured, including word-level variables — written frequency and spoken frequency (British National Corpus, BNC Consortium, 2007), age of acquisition in native children (Kuperman, 2012), number of syllables, number of neighbours with doublet spelling — and consonant-level variables — type of consonant (p, t, k), consonant position (pre- or post-stress). CC:C ratios were lowest with the consonant [k] and highest with [t] ($p < .001$; see Figure 4.3), as in Italian (Esposito & Di Benedetto, 1999). The analysis of the dataset did not reveal other effects of interest. Future research could investigate these variables again and also include other potentially impactful variables (see Repetti, 2009; Hamann & Colombo, 2017). Finally, looking at tasks, the project did not aim at comparing production tasks that provide orthographic input with purely oral ones, but the preliminary study found no differences between word repetition tasks with and without orthographic input (Bassetti, 2017; see Question 1b given earlier for details).

In conclusion, it appears that some variables related to L1 phonology (sounds, phonotactics) and the L1 lexicon (cognates) can impact the level of orthography-induced gemination, but more research is needed to reach firm conclusions.

L+ speech production: Summary of findings

The four production studies reported earlier confirmed that Italian$_{L1}$ speakers make a contrast between singleton and geminate consonants in English$_{L+}$. They produce the same consonant as shorter in words where it is spelled with a letter and longer in words where it is spelled with a doublet, for instance, producing a longer [t] in *kitty* than in *city*. This is not simply a difference in sound duration but evidence of a phonological contrast. There is both descriptive and experimental evidence for this statement. First, Italians use consonant duration to distinguish English homophones such as *finish-Finnish*, such that they realise English orthographic minimal pairs as phonological minimal pairs distinguished by one phoneme: A singleton [n] in *finish* and a geminate [nː] in *Finnish*. Second, there is no overlap between the durations of the two categories (see Figure 4.3).

This long-short contrast occurs because the orthographic inventory of English grapheme-phoneme correspondences in Italians' minds features a <CC>=/Cː/ (doublet = geminate consonant) correspondence, influenced by Italians' grapheme-phoneme correspondences, which results in the presence of gemination in their English$_{L+}$ phonological inventory. Geminates are not twice as long as singletons, as in their Italian production (see comparison

Effects of orthography on L+ speech production 61

in Bassetti et al., 2018), but about 50% longer than singletons. A number of variables modulate this effect, including naturalistic exposure, as sequential bilinguals have lower ratios than instructed learners; proficiency level, which is related to lower levels of gemination; short-term memory, which reduces ratios in bilinguals; type of consonant, as [t] has the highest ratios; and L1 phonotactics, with higher ratios in intervocalic than other positions.

Having found that Italians make a length contrast in English$_{L+}$, the next question was then whether they believe that the English language has a length contrast.

References

Bassetti, B. (2017). Orthography affects second language speech: Double letters and geminate production in English. *Journal of Experimental Psychology: Learning, Memory, and Cognition, 43*(11), 1835–1842. https://doi.org/10.1037/xlm0000417

Bassetti, B., & Atkinson, N. (2015). Effects of orthographic forms on pronunciation in experienced instructed second language learners. *Applied Psycholinguistics, 36*, 67–91. https://doi.org/10.1017/S0142716414000435

Bassetti, B., Mairano, P., Masterson, J., & Cerni, T. (2020). Effects of orthographic forms on phonological awareness and speech production in second language speakers, with consideration of speaker variables. *Language Learning, 70*(4), *1218–1256*. doi:10.1111/lang.12423

Bassetti, B., Sokolović-Perović, M., Mairano, P., & Cerni, T. (2018). Orthography-induced length contrasts in the second language phonological systems of L2 speakers of English: Evidence from minimal pairs. *Language and Speech, 61*(4), 577–597. doi:10.1177/0023830918780141 PMID:29914283

BNC Consortium. (2007). *The British national corpus, XML edition*. Oxford Text Archive. http://hdl.handle.net/20.500.12024/2554

Esposito, A., & Di Benedetto, M. G. (1999). Acoustical and perceptual study of gemination in Italian stops. *Journal of the Acoustical Society of America, 106*(4), 2051–2062. https://doi.org/10.1121/1.428056

Hamann, S., & Colombo, I. E. (2017). A formal account of the interaction of orthography and perception. *Natural Language & Linguistic Theory, 35*(3), 683–714. https://doi.org/10.1007/s11049-017-9362-3

Iwashita, N., Brown, A., McNamara, T., & O'Hagan, S. (2008). Assessed levels of second language speaking proficiency: How distinct? *Applied Linguistics, 29*(24–49). https://doi.org/10.1093/applin/amm017

Kuperman, V., Stadthagen-Gonzalez, H., & Brysbaert, M. (2012). Age-of-acquisition ratings for 30,000 English words. *Behavior Research Methods, 44*(4), 978–990. https://doi.org/10.3758/s13428-012-0210-4

Mairano, P., Santiago, F. N., & Delais-Roussarie, E. (2018). *Gémination non native en français d'apprenants italophones [Non-native gemination in Italian-speaking learners of French]* Actes des Journées d'Etudes sur la Parole (JEP), Aix-en-Provence, France.

Repetti, L. (2009). Gemination in English loans in American varieties of Italian. In A. Calabrese & L. Wetzels (Eds.), *Loan phonology* (pp. 225–240). John Benjamins.

Shea, C. (2017). L1 English/L2 Spanish: Orthography–phonology activation without contrasts. *Second Language Research, 33*(2), 207–232. https://doi.org/10.1177/0267658316684905

5 Effects of orthography on L+ awareness, perception, and learning

Having established that Italians produce geminates in English$_{L+}$ speech in Chapter 4, this chapter reports findings related to gemination in speech perception, awareness, and learning. Each section opens with a research question (listed in Table 3.1) and a summary of the findings, then presents more detailed descriptions. Experiments are summarised with a table illustrating the design and one presenting predictions and results.

L+ awareness: Consonant categorisation

Question 4: Do Italian$_{L1}$ speakers categorise the same English consonant as singleton or geminate, depending on its spelling?

Yes. Italian$_{L1}$ speakers of English$_{L+}$ — learners and sequential bilinguals — categorise English consonants as belonging to two separate phonological categories: Singletons if spelled with a letter or geminates if spelled with a doublet, therefore rejecting rhymes where the same consonant is spelled with one or two letters, such as *very-cherry*, and erroneously believing that English rhyming words such as *very* and *merry* do not rhyme because *merry* is 'long' or 'double', in line with the Italian non-rhyming word pair *caro-carro*.

Given that Italians produce singleton and geminate consonants in English words, even in minimal pairs, do they actually think that English has singletons and geminates? Experiment 2 in Bassetti et al. (2020) tested whether Italians categorise the same consonant as two different consonants in two words that are spelled with a letter or doublet. To clarify participants' thinking, qualitative data was elicited from them after the experiment in an open format.

Table 5.1 shows the design. Participants performed a Rhyme Judgment Task, whereby the screen displayed two written English words and participants answered whether the words rhymed or not by pressing a button. The targets were C-CC rhymes — rhymes where the same consonant was spelled with a letter or doublet, such as /ˈskɒlə/ -/ˈdɒlə/ (*scholar-dollar*) If Italians believe

DOI: 10.4324/9780429343117-5

Table 5.1 Design, Experiment 2, Bassetti et al. (2020).

Methods			Design	
Participants	Materials	Task	IV	DV
75 natives, 77 bilinguals, 96 learners (Exp. 1 participants, minus lost data)	12 C-CC rhymes (*very-cherry*), 24 controls (12 heterographic rhymes: *lie-cry*, 12 non-rhyming pairs: *fox-blogs*)	Rhyme judgment	Language background (between: Natives, bilinguals, learners) * type of word pair (within: Controls, C-CC rhymes)	Accuracy (correct, incorrect)

that English has contrastive consonant length, they should not consider such pairs as rhymes, thinking that they contain two different consonants — a singleton and a geminate. This would reflect their behaviour with Italian, given that none of them considered the Italian word pair *caro-carro* as a rhyme in a subsequent Italian rhyme judgment task. Controls included heterographic rhymes (rhymes with differences in spelling other than consonant number, such as /laɪ/ — /kraɪ/, *lie-cry*) and non-rhyming word pairs (/fɒks/ — /blɒgz/, *fox-blogs*). To test whether naturalistic exposure reduces OEs on awareness, the experiment compared sequential bilinguals and learners.

Results. As the percentages of correct answers in Figure 5.1 show, the L+ speakers (learners and bilinguals) rejected C-CC rhymes.

Table 5.2 summarises the results. The final model, *ACCURACY ~ PAIR_TYPE * GROUP + (PAIR_TYPE|PARTICIPANT) + (1|WORD_PAIR)*, revealed an interaction between language background and type of word pair ($\chi^2 = 24.72, p < .001$), meaning that group differences in probability of answering correctly varied across types of word pairs. Pairwise comparisons for each group revealed that learners were more likely to answer correctly with control pairs than with C-CC rhymes, $p = .037$, whereas there was no difference in the bilingual group, $p = 0.208$.

To summarise, the Rhyme Judgment task revealed that Italian learners reject English$_{L+}$ rhymes where the same consonant is spelled with a letter in one word and a doublet in the other one. Qualitative data was then elicited to clarify why Italians rejected these rhymes, with the prediction that they would state that English distinguishes short and long consonants.

Qualitative data. All participants read aloud the words *very* and *merry*, stated whether they rhymed or not, and explained the reasons for their

Effects of orthography on L+ awareness, perception and learning 65

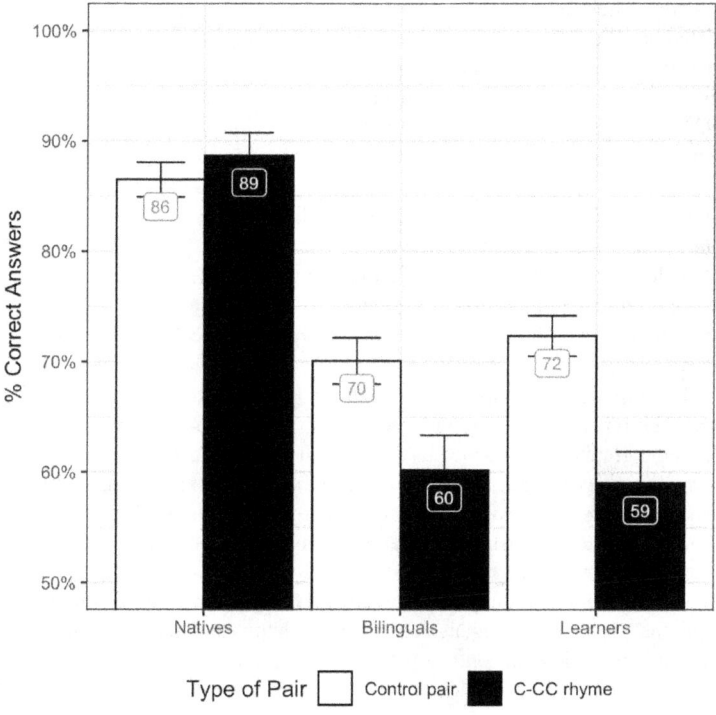

Figure 5.1 Mean percentage of correct answers in the Rhyme Judgment Task.

Note: Heterographic rhymes and non-rhyming pairs are merged for clarity, as differences were minimal.

Table 5.2 Predictions and results, Experiment 2, Bassetti et al. (2020).

Predictions	Results
1.a L+ speakers: The correct answer is more likely with control than a C-CC pair	✓ L+ speakers' percent correct: controls = 71%, C-CC = 60%
1.b Natives: No difference in accuracy between C-CC and controls	✓ Natives: Controls = 86%, C-CC = 89%, Accuracy likelihood with C-CC vs. control pairs: $p = 0.288$
2. OE (lower accuracy likelihood with C-CC than control pairs) stronger in learners than bilinguals	✓ Accuracy likelihood with C-CC vs. control pairs: Learners: $p = 0.037$ Bilinguals: $p = 0.208$

answers. Their audio-recorded answers were transcribed and coded. As predicted, all English$_{L1}$ speakers stated that *very-merry* is a rhyme, whereas the majority of Italians said that it is not. The percentages of rejections were very similar among learners and bilinguals (78% and 73%, respectively). Most (92%) explained that the [r] in *merry* is 'double', 'long', or 'stronger/harsher'. Representative answers (translated) include:

The *r* [in *merry*] has a stronger sound, it's like the double in Italian. (BL34)
Merry has the double and *very* doesn't. (ESL36)
They don't rhyme because *merry* is longer than *very*. (BL67)
In the pronunciation of *merry*, one can strongly hear the double *r* (BL64)
I pronounce *r-r-y* stronger; I pronounce the *r* in *very* weaker. (ESL32).

To compare their thinking about gemination in English and in Italian, Italians then repeated the task with the Italian words *caro-carro*, which contain the same graphemes <r>-<rr> as the English words. Most respondents (93%) correctly answered that this is not a rhyme because [r] and [rː] have different lengths (that is to say, are different consonants). This shows that Italians hold similar views of English and Italian CC-consonants, considering both geminates, and for the same reasons.

In conclusion, both experimental and qualitative data showed that Italians think that the English language contrasts singletons and geminates and represents this phonological contrast with the orthographic contrast <C>-<CC>, as their first language Italian does.

L+ speech perception

Given that Italians think that English has geminate and singleton consonants, corresponding to doublet and letter spellings, the next question was: Do they hold this belief in spite of perceiving no durational differences in English$_{L1}$ speakers' speech, or do they actually perceive durational differences — corresponding to singleton and geminate consonants — when listening to English$_{L1}$ speech? This section presents two experiments that investigated whether Italians perceive durational differences — corresponding to geminate and singleton consonants — when listening to English words.

Question 5: Do Italian$_{L1}$ listeners perceive the same English$_{L+}$ consonant as singleton versus geminate, depending on its spelling?

Yes. Italian$_{L1}$ listeners of English$_{L+}$ — learners and sequential bilinguals — illusorily perceive geminate consonants in spoken English words that are spelled with a doublet, because if their mental representation of an English$_{L+}$ word contains a (orthography-induced) geminate they illusorily

Effects of orthography on L+ awareness, perception and learning 67

perceive longer duration in an English$_{L1}$ speaker's production of that word, for instance reporting that two audio recordings of [fɪnɪʃ] contain different sounds if they think that one is a recording of *finish* and the other a recording of *Finnish*.

Given that Italians think that English has geminate and singleton consonants, corresponding to doublet and letter spellings, do they also perceive durational differences — corresponding to geminate and singleton consonants — when listening to spoken English?

Question 5a: Does orthographic form affect English$_{L+}$ consonant perception in Italian$_{L1}$- English$_{L+}$ bilinguals?

If Italians perceive illusory durational differences in spoken English$_{L+}$ consonants, when they hear two homophonic English words that are spelled with <C> or <CC>, they should perceive the same spoken consonant as a singleton or geminate. For instance, they should perceive the [n] consonant as singleton [n] in *finish* and as geminate [n:] in *Finnish*.

A Consonant Perception Task was especially devised to measure the discrimination of spurious consonant length using the same/different responses to pairs of homophonic word pairs. All participants listened to native speakers' recordings of homophonic word pairs, for instance [fɪnɪʃ] and [fɪnɪʃ], and decided whether the two words contained the same sounds (correct answer) or different sounds (incorrect answer).

As Table 5.3 shows, there were four groups of 25 participants each. Two groups of 50 English$_{L1}$ speakers and 50 Italian$_{L1}$-English$_{L+}$ bilinguals were each divided into two groups: The Auditory Input (AI) group listened to the pairs of homophones; the Auditory-Visual Input (AVI) group saw two pictures that activated the two target words in their mental lexicon before listening to the words. Figure 5.2 illustrates the two groups' tasks with the example of the *finish-Finnish* pair. Both groups listened to [fɪnɪʃ] twice, but for the AOI group, a picture of a finish-line flag was used to activate the word *finish*, and a picture of the Finnish flag was used to activate the word *Finnish*.

The targets were 18 C-CC homophonic word pairs, such as *finish-Finnish* (16 were later used to study minimal pair production; see Question 2 in Chapter 4). The control pairs were homonyms, that is to say, words with the same phonological and orthographic form but different meaning, such as *palm* (tree) — *palm* (part of hand). Thirty filler pairs containing two different consonants (*angle-ankle*) were used to vary the response patterns. After the perception task, a Word Spelling Task checked participants' knowledge of all words in C-CC and control pairs (the same task used in the production study; see Question 1c in Chapter 4). If either word in a pair was spelled incorrectly, the whole pair was eliminated from analysis, as no OEs were expected.

68 *Effects of orthography on L+ awareness, perception and learning*

Table 5.3 Design, Experiment 1, Bassetti et al. (2021).

Methods			Design	
Participants	Materials	Task	IV	DV
Natives, bilinguals (each n = 50; each divided in two groups: Auditory input and auditory-visual input)	18 C-CC homophonic word pairs (*finish-Finnish*); 18 control pairs (homonyms: *palm-palm*)	Consonant perception	Language background (between: Natives, bilinguals, learners) * type of input (between: Auditory, auditory-visual) * type of word pair (within: Controls, C-CC homophones)	Accuracy (correct, incorrect)

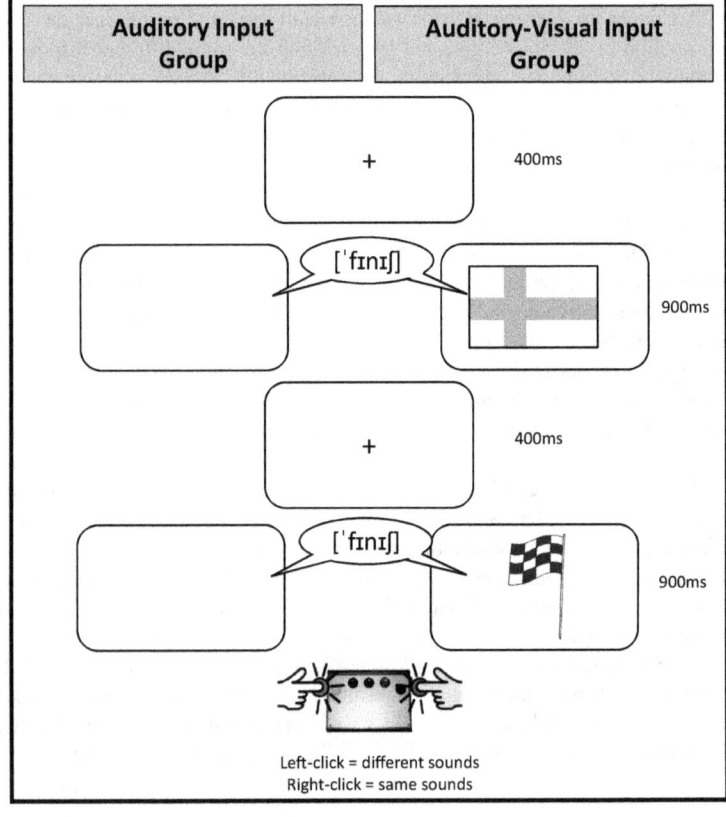

Figure 5.2 Schematic of the perception experiment.

Effects of orthography on L+ awareness, perception and learning 69

Table 5.4 shows the predictions. If orthographic form affects perception, when bilinguals hear [fɪnɪʃ], they should perceive a singleton [n] if they think they are hearing *finish* and a geminate [nː] if they think they are hearing *Finnish*. However, this effect should only occur if they know which words they are hearing; hence, only bilinguals in the AVI group were expected to be affected. That is to say, AI bilinguals, who heard [fɪnɪʃ] twice, should perceive two words with the same phonological form; AVI bilinguals, who heard [fɪnɪʃ] twice but thought they were hearing *finish* and *Finnish*, should perceive a singleton and a geminate, respectively, and therefore incorrectly think they heard words with a difference in sound. This would be due to top-down interference of the two words' mental representations (possibly also reinforced by co-activation of the two words' orthographic forms). Natives should always answer correctly.

The right-most bar in Figure 5.3 shows that — as predicted — bilinguals who received visual input often answered C-CC pairs incorrectly, meaning that they perceived different consonants in C- and CC-homophones.

Table 5.5 summarises the results. The final model, *ACCURACY ~ LANGUAGE_BACKGROUND * PAIR_TYPE * INPUT_TYPE + (PAIR_TYPE|PARTICIPANT) + (INPUT_TYPE|WORD_PAIR)*, revealed a three-way interaction of language background, type of input, and type of word pair ($\chi^2 = 4.19$, $p = 0.041$), and post-hocs confirmed that bilinguals who had received visual input were more likely to perceive different sounds in C-CC pairs than control pairs.

Table 5.4 Predictions, Experiment 1, Bassetti et al. (2021).

Language Background	Auditory Input		Auditory-Visual input	
	Controls	C-CC homophones	Controls	C-CC homophones
	/pɑːm/- /pɑːm/	/ˈfɪnɪʃ/-/ˈfɪnɪʃ/	/pɑːm/-/pɑːm/ 🌴 ✋	/ˈfɪnɪʃ/-/ˈfɪnɪʃ/ 🏁 ➕
Natives	✓	✓	✓	✓
Bilinguals	✓	✓	✓	✗ (\<C\>=/C/; \<CC\>=/Cː/)

Note: ✓ = correct answer; ✗ = incorrect answer.

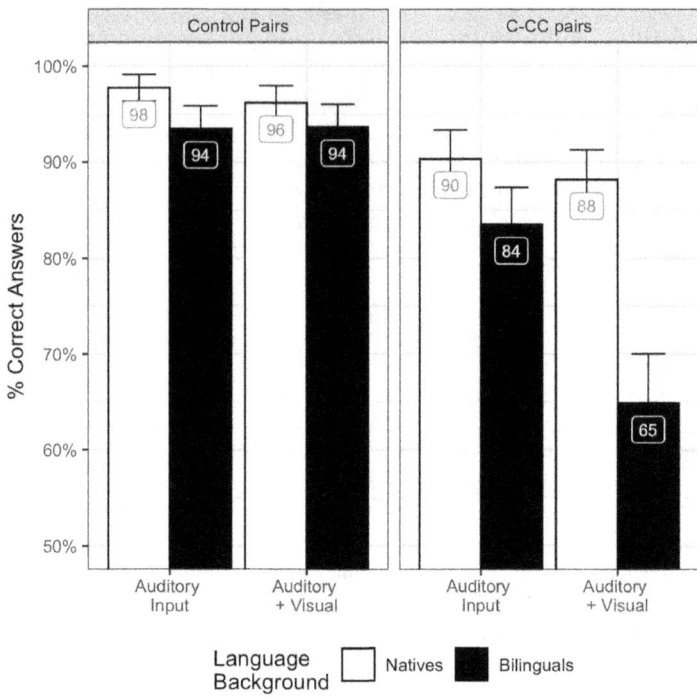

Figure 5.3 Mean percentage of correct answers, Experiment 1, Bassetti et al. (2021).

Table 5.5 Predictions and results, Experiment 1, Bassetti et al. (2021).

Predictions	Results
1.a Bilinguals with auditory-visual input: Correct answer more likely with control pairs than C-CC pairs	✓ $p < 0.001$
1.b Bilinguals with auditory input: Same likelihood of correct answer with C-CC and control pairs	✓ $p = 0.209$
1.c Natives: Same likelihood of correct answer regardless of type of pair and type of input	✓ AI natives: $p = 0.135$; AVI natives: $p = 0.153$
2. C-CC pairs: Incorrect answers are more likely in bilinguals with AVI input than in any other group	✓ AVI bilinguals: vs. AI bilinguals, $p = 0.030$ vs. natives, $p < 0.001$

Results confirm that consonant spelling affects Italian$_{L1}$ bilinguals' English$_{L+}$ speech perception, as they perceive the same spoken consonant inside the recordings of two spoken homophonic words as a singleton or a geminate because of its C- or CC-spelling, but only following semantic activation of the two words (by means of pictures). Bilinguals who heard the same recordings without knowing which two words they were hearing did not perceive different sounds.

Question 5b: Does naturalistic exposure eliminate or reduce orthography-induced gemination in perception?

Having established that orthographic forms affect speech perception in bilinguals, the next question was: Are there differences between instructed learners and bilinguals? This is because extensive naturalistic exposure could reduce OEs in perception. Experiment 2 in Bassetti et al. (2021) then compared learners, bilinguals, and native speakers performing the Consonant Perception Task with Auditory-Visual Input. Table 5.6 shows the design.

The two rightmost bars in Figure 5.4 show that both bilinguals and learners had low mean percentages of correct answers with C-CC homophones, and bilinguals were just above chance level. With control pairs, all participants performed at ceiling level.

Table 5.7 summarises the results. The final model, *ACCURACY ~ LANGUAGE_BACKGROUND * PAIR_TYPE + (PAIR_TYPE|PARTICIPANT) + (1|WORDPAIR)*, revealed an interaction of language background and type of word pair ($\chi^2 = 16.33$, $p < 0.001$). Contrasts confirmed that L+ listeners were more likely to correctly answer correctly control pairs than C-CC pairs. Native listener control pairs than C-CC pairs. Native listeners were equally correct with both pair types. Contrary to predictions, learners outperformed bilinguals.

Table 5.6 Design, Experiment 2, Bassetti et al. (2021).

Methods			Design	
Participants	Materials	Task	IV	DV
Natives, bilinguals, and learners (each $n = 30$)	As Experiment 1: 18 C-CC homophonic word pairs; 18 control pairs (homonyms)	Consonant perception with auditory-visual input	Language background (between: Natives, bilinguals, learners) *type of word pair (within: Controls, C-CC homophones)	Accuracy (correct, incorrect)

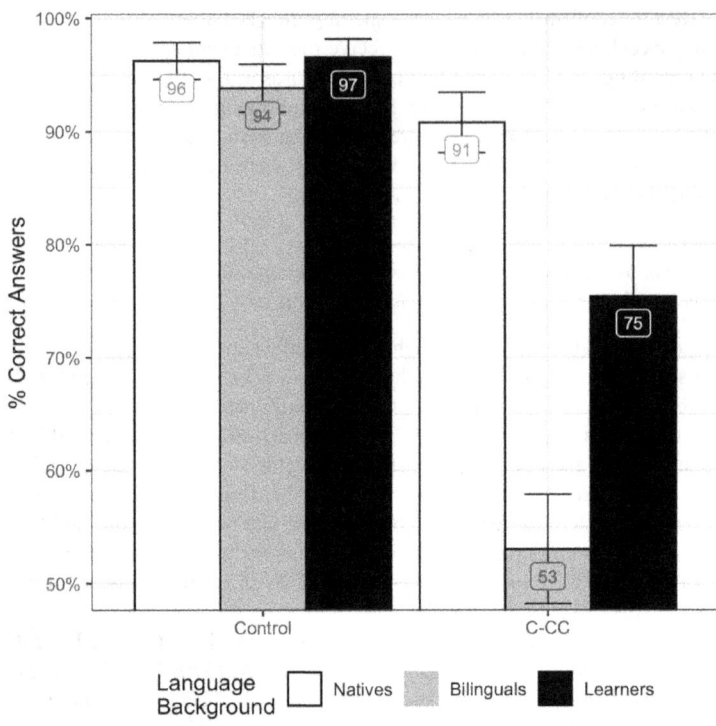

Figure 5.4 Mean percentage of correct answers, Experiment 2, Bassetti et al. (2021).

Table 5.7 Predictions and results, Experiment 2, Bassetti et al. (2021).

Predictions	Results
1.a L+ listeners: Correct answer more likely with control than C-CC pairs	✓ $p < 0.001$
1.b Natives: No difference between C-CC and controls	✓ $p = 0.117$
2. Stronger effects (lower likelihood of accuracy with C-CC rhymes) in learners than in bilinguals	✗ Stronger effects in bilinguals than learners, $p = 0.011$

Discussion

The two perception experiments showed that Italian$_{L1}$ listeners perceive a long-short contrast in English$_{L+}$ that is unattested in the phonological systems of English$_{L1}$ speakers, as reflected in natives' performance in the task. In both experiments, Italian$_{L1}$-English$_{L+}$ listeners perceived different consonants — a singleton or a geminate — in spoken English homophonous words, with illusory durational differences on the basis of the consonant's orthographic form containing a letter or a doublet. This only happened after the semantic activation of two homophones spelled with a letter or doublet, not if listeners heard the same two recordings without previous activation of the two homophones.

This is then a top-down effect, as Italians' mental representation of an English word contains an orthography-induced geminate, and this geminate in their mental word representation interferes with speech perception, resulting in the illusory perception of longer duration in the auditory input. Indeed, Experiment 1 confirms that this effect is post-lexical, that is to say, Italians only perceive geminates after accessing their mental representation of the target word. Bilinguals were affected if the C-word and CC-word had been semantically activated by pictures, but not without lexical activation. The experiment did not provide participants any orthographic input, confirming that geminates are present in listeners' mental representations. It cannot be ruled out that the word's orthographic representation is also activated during speech perception and affects it. Further research could investigate the time course of these effects in order to clarify their origin.

Naturalistic exposure did not reduce the effect, as both sequential bilinguals and instructed learners were likely to perceive C-CC pairs as containing different sounds. On the contrary, bilinguals' accuracy with C-CC pairs was very low compared with their almost ceiling-level performance with control pairs, and in Experiment 2 it was just above chance level. The contrary-to-predictions stronger effect in bilinguals than learners is probably an artifact of sample and/or materials selection. The 30 learners who could spell enough words to be included in the study were less than a third of those who had taken the test, and had higher proficiency, vocabulary size and exposure to auditory input than the other learners (Bassetti et al., 2021). If this is the reason, future research may find stronger OEs in learners by including only frequent words and testing more typical learners. However, the stronger OE in bilinguals may well be a genuine effect, as some previous studies (Simonchyk & Darcy, 2018; Veivo et al., 2016) also found stronger OEs on perception in more advanced L+ listeners than less experienced ones. This could be because phonological representations need to be ingrained before they affect perception. The impact of naturalistic exposure and proficiency on OEs in perception should be further investigated.

Bringing it all together: The perception-production-awareness connection

The main aim of this project was to investigate for the first time all aspects of the orthography-phonology relationship at once — perception, production, lexical learning, and phonological learning. This was the main reason for running a larger-than-usual project on OEs, collecting data from various different tasks from the same English$_{L+}$ speakers (the other reason was to collect enough data to investigate OE predictors, see Question 3 in Chapter 4). The studies reported earlier individually revealed that word spelling affects speech perception, production, and awareness. The question was: Are these phenomena all related?

Question 6: Is there a correlation between perception, production, and categorisation of geminates in English$_{L+}$?

Yes. Higher levels of awareness that English has no contrastive consonants (higher awareness accuracy scores) were associated with higher levels of consonant perception (perception accuracy scores) and with lower levels of geminate production (lower CC:C ratios).

Bassetti et al. (2020) reported preliminary findings of a link between higher phonological awareness and weaker OEs in speech production. Higher levels of awareness that English has no contrastive consonant length (better performance on the C-CC rhyming task) were associated with lower levels of gemination in production (lower CC:C ratios). After completing the analysis of the whole project's dataset, it became possible to bring all results together and run a correlation analysis of the magnitudes of OEs on production, perception, and awareness across all 180 Italian$_{L1}$ speakers of English$_{L+}$.

The new correlation analysis revealed that higher levels of awareness were associated with both higher levels of perception accuracy ($r = 0.14, p < 0.001$) and lower levels of gemination in production (lower CC:C ratio, $r = -0.11$, $p < 0.001$). That is to say, those who categorised consonants as geminate or singleton were also more likely to produce and perceive geminates. The correlations were weak, and there was no correlation between perception and production ($r < 0.10$). This could be due to various reasons, including high levels of individual variation or the relatively small number (30) of learners who completed the perception task.

The relationship among OEs on perception, production, and awareness should be further investigated, but these preliminary findings point in the right direction, showing that the same orthographic form has similar effects on different aspects of L+ phonology. The most likely reason is that orthographic forms affect L+ speakers' phonological representations of L+ words, which are then reflected in production, perception, and awareness.

L+ learning

The final two questions investigated the potential effects of orthography on two aspects of L+ learning: Lexical learning — specifically, learning the phonological form of new words — and phonological learning — specifically learning about L+ consonants.

Question 7: Lexical learning: Do Italian$_{L1}$ speakers learn new spoken English words as containing a geminate if spelled with a doublet?

Yes. Experienced Italian$_{L1}$ learners of English$_{L+}$ learn a new spoken English word as containing a geminate if they saw the word spelled with a consonant doublet, and as a singleton if they saw a single-letter consonant spelling, for instance learning the pseudoword [prɪnɪʃ] as [prɪnɪʃ] if they saw the spelling <prinish> and as [prɪn:ɪʃ] if they saw the spelling <prinnish>. Those who saw no word spellings learn some words as containing a singleton and others as containing a geminate (with consonants that can geminate in the L1 and can be spelled with doublets in the L+). Orthography-induced consonants are found in both speech production and awareness (rhyme judgment) tasks.

Having shown that orthographic forms affect L+ speech production, perception, and awareness, the next question was: Are OEs established when L+ learners first learn a word, or do such effects emerge later as a result of repeated exposure? More specifically, when experienced L+ learners learn a new spoken L+ word, do they learn that the word contains a geminate if they see that the word is spelled with a doublet?

To establish this, a study led by Tania Cerni (Cerni et al., 2019) compared Italian$_{L1}$ learners of English$_{L+}$ who learnt new English$_{L+}$ spoken words from auditory input only (the Auditory Input group) or from both auditory and orthographic input (the Auditory-Orthographic Input group). Table 5.8 shows the design. All participants learnt a set of spoken pseudowords, which were created by replacing the initial consonant(s) of a pair of C-CC homophones, for instance, [prɪnɪʃ] was created from *finish-Finnish*. In the Auditory-Orthographic input group, half of the participants learnt the spoken

Table 5.8 Design, Cerni et al. (2019).

Methods			Design	
Participants	Materials	Task	IV	DV
Two groups of learners: Auditory input; Auditory-Orthographic input (n = 24 each)	Pairs of lexical items: $CC_{pseudoword}$-C_{word} targets, $C_{pseudoword}$-C_{word} controls, CC_{word}-$C_{pseudoword}$ controls (10 each)	**Exp. 1:** Picture naming **Exp. 2:** Rhyme judgment	Group (between: AI, AOI)* type of word pair (within: CC_{pw}-C_w target, C_{pw}-C_w control, C_w-CC_{pw} control)	**Exp. 1:** CC:C ratio **Exp. 2:** Accuracy (correct, incorrect)

76 Effects of orthography on L+ awareness, perception and learning

pseudoword together with a C-spelling (<prinish>), and half learnt it with a CC-spelling (<prinnish>). The materials also included real English words.

If orthography affects lexical learning, AOI participants should learn new English$_{L+}$ words (pseudowords) as containing a geminate if they see a CC-spelling and as containing a singleton if they see a C-spelling. Learners only exposed to auditory input should learn all words as containing a singleton if they perceive native English consonants as singletons, or they should learn some words with a singleton and some with a geminate if they perceive native English consonants as in-between a singleton and a geminate.

Figure 5.5 illustrates the learning session. During an individual one-hour session, each student learnt 25 pairings of a picture (unusual animals/objects)

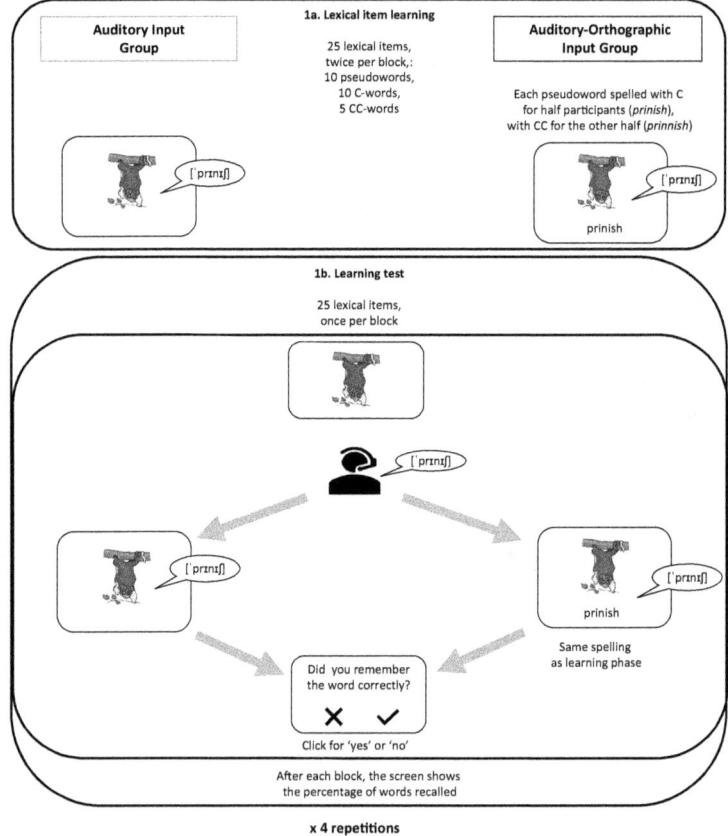

Figure 5.5 The learning session.

Effects of orthography on L+ awareness, perception and learning 77

and a lexical item (word or pseudoword), Their knowledge of the lexical items was tested using the production and awareness tasks from Bassetti et al. (2020).

Figure 5.6 shows the testing session. Both speech production and awareness were tested, to see whether the OEs already found with known words in Bassetti et al. (2020) would show in words that had just been learnt. The final spelling task tested whether the AOI group had learnt the correct spelling, and whether the AI group had perceived and therefore learnt a singleton or geminate consonant in the new spoken words they had heard.

Question 7a: Are newly learned CC-words produced with a geminate?

In the picture naming task (2a in Figure 5.6), participants orally produced all lexical items (pseudowords and words). In order to measure gemination,

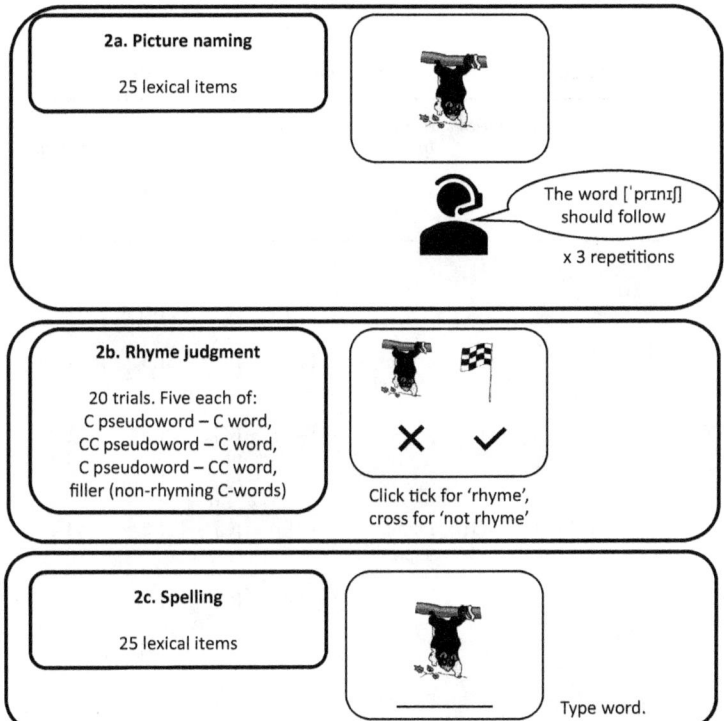

Figure 5.6 The testing session: Production, awareness, and spelling tasks.

for each pair of lexical items, a consonant ratio was obtained by dividing the duration of the target consonant in the first word by its duration in the second word. Predictions differed by type of word pair, as shown in the Predicted Consonant Ratios column in Table 5.9. For instance, for $CC_{pseudoword}$-C_{word} pairs (first row), we predicted a ratio of 1.6 for the AOI group, as follows: Having seen the spelling <prinnish>, the AOI learners should produce a geminate in *prinnish* and a singleton in *finish*. Since Italians' English$_{L+}$ geminates are about 1.6 times as long as corresponding singletons, the ratio should be about 1.6. In the AI group, if Italians perceive all English consonants as singletons, the consonant ratio should be 1, as the consonant *prinnish* should be as long as in *finish*. However, if they perceive English consonants as in-between a singleton and a geminate, some AI participants should produce the pseudoword with a singleton and some with a geminate, so the ratio for these pairs should be in-between 1 and 1.6.

The rightmost column of Table 5.9 shows results (geometric means of first-word:second-word consonant ratios). In the AVI group, those who had

Table 5.9 Predicted and observed word-pair ratios, Cerni et al. (2019).

Type of Pair	Example	Group	Written Input	Predicted target consonant		First:second consonant ratio	
				First word	Second word	Predicted	Observed
CC_{pw} C_{word}		AI	-	[C] or [C, C:]	[C]	1 or 1–1.6	1.35
	[prɪnɪʃ]-[fɪnɪʃ]	AOI	prinnish-finish	[C:]	[C]	1.6	1.64
CC_{word} C_{pw}		AI	-	[C:]	[C] or [C]/[C:]	1.6 or 1–1.6	1.14
	[fɪnɪʃ]-[prɪnɪʃ]	AOI	Finnish-prinish	[C:]	[C]	1.6	1.47
C_{pw} C_{word}		AI	-	[C] or [C, C:]	[C]	1 or 1–1.6	1.30
	[prɪnɪʃ]-[fɪnɪʃ]	AOI	prinish-finish	[C]	[C]	1	1.13

seen a new word spelled with a doublet consistently produced it with a geminate, and those who had seen the same word spelled with a letter produced it with a singleton.

The final model, *RATIO_LOG ~ LEARNING_GROUP * PAIR_TYPE + (PAIR_TYPE|PARTICIPANT) + (1|WORDPAIR)*, and post-hoc tests (see Table 5.10) showed that the AOI group had produced CC-pseudowords with a geminate, as $CC_{pseudoword}$-C_{word} and CC_{word}-$C_{pseudoword}$ pairs had similar ratios ($p > 0.05$), and both these CC-C pairs had higher ratio than $C_{pseudoword}$-C_{word} pairs (both $p < 0.01$). The AI group had similar ratios across types of pairs because they produced some pseudowords with a geminate and some with a singleton.

Table 5.10 Predictions and results, Experiment 1, Cerni et al. (2019).

Predictions	Results
1.a AOI group: higher ratio in CC-C pairs than C-C pairs	✓ $CC_{pseudoword}$-C_{word} vs. C-C: $p < 0.001$ ✓ CC_{word}-$C_{pseudoword}$ vs. C-C: $p = 0.004$
similar ratio in the two types of CC-C pairs	✓ CC_{word}-$C_{pseudoword}$ vs. $CC_{pseudoword}$-C_{word}: $p = 0.530$
1.b AI group: Ratio similar across types of pairs	✓ $CC_{pseudoword}$-C_{word} vs. C-C: $p = 0.993$ ✓ CC_{word}-$C_{pseudoword}$ vs. C-C: $p = 0.700$ ✓ CC_{word}-$C_{pseudoword}$ vs. $CC_{pseudoword}$-C_{word}: $p = 0.211$
2.a CC-C pairs (CC_{word}-$C_{pseudoword}$, $CC_{pseudoword}$-C_{word}): Ratio higher in AOI than AI group	✓ both $p < 0.001$
2.b C-C pairs: Ratio higher in AI than AOI group	✓ $p = 0.049$

Question 7b: Are consonants in newly learned CC-words categorised as geminates?

To test whether participants thought that the newly learned words contained a geminate, they performed a rhyme judgment task (2b in Figure 5.6) similar to the one used with real words by Bassetti et al. (2020). Table 5.11 shows predicted and observed mean percentages of correct answers. Looking at the first row, for a pair containing a CC-pseudoword and a C-word, for AOI participants the predicted mean accuracy was 60%, in line with mean accuracy with CC-C rhymes in the awareness task in Bassetti et al. (2020). As for AI participants, if they learn CC-pseudowords with a singleton, they would

Table 5.11 Predicted and observed mean percentages of correct answers, Cerni et al. (2019).

Type of Pair	Example	Group	Written Input	Predicted consonants	Accuracy Predicted	Observed
CC_{pw} C_{word} [prɪnɪʃ]-[fɪnɪʃ]		AI	-	[n—n] = ✓ or [n—n] = ✓; [nː—n] = ✘	100% or 60%-100%	69%
		AOI	prinnish-finish	[nː—n] = ✘	60%	69%
CC_{word} C_{pw} [fɪnɪʃ]-[prɪnɪʃ]		AI	-	[nː—n] = ✘ or [nː—n] = ✘; [nː—nː] = ✓	60% or 60%-100%	87%
		AOI	Finnish-prinish	[nː—n] = ✘	60%	64%
C_{pw} C_{word} [prɪnɪʃ]-[fɪnɪʃ]		AI	-	[n—n] = ✓ or [n—n] = ✓; [nː—n] = ✘	100% or 60%-100%	77%
		AOI	prinish-finish	[n—n] = ✓	100%	93%

correctly consider [prɪnɪʃ]-[fɪnɪʃ] as a rhyme. However, if they learn about half of CC-pseudowords with a singleton and about half with a geminate, they should judge just above half of such pairs as CC-C pairs (predicted accuracy = 60%) and the rest as C-C pairs (predicted accuracy = 100%), ending up with an accuracy of about 80%.

As Table 5.12 shows, learners were likely to think that a newly learned spoken word contained a geminate consonant if they had seen the word spelled with a doublet. The final model, *ACCURACY ~ LEARNING_GROUP * PAIR_TYPE + (PAIR_TYPE|PARTICIPANT) + (1|WORDPAIR)*, and post-hoc tests showed that the AOI group thought that newly learned CC-pseudowords contained a geminate, hence rejecting CC_{pw}-C_w and CC_w-C_{pw} rhymes and accepting C_{pw}-C_w rhymes. The AI group was equally likely to correctly answer all types of pairs.

Table 5.12 Predictions and results, Experiment 2, Cerni et al. (2019).

Predictions	Results
1.a AOI group: correct answer more likely with C-C pairs than with CC-C pairs	✓ CC_{word}-$C_{pseudoword}$ vs. C-C: $p = 0.002$ ✓ $CC_{pseudoword}$-C_{word} vs. C-C: $p = 0.002$
similar ratio in CC-C pairs	✓ CC_{word}-$C_{pseudoword}$ vs. $CC_{pseudoword}$-C_{word}: $p = 0.982$
1.b AI group: Correct answer equally likely across types of pairs	✓ $CC_{pseudoword}$-C_{word} vs. C-C: $p = 0.872$ ✓ CC_{word}-$C_{pseudoword}$ vs. C-C: $p = 0.736$ ✗ CC_{word}-$C_{pseudoword}$ vs. $CC_{pseudoword}$-C_{word}: $p = 0.04$
2.a CC-C pairs (CC_{word}-$C_{pseudoword}$, $CC_{pseudoword}$-C_{word}): Correct answer more likely in AI group than AOI group	✗ $CC_{pseudoword}$-C_{word}: $p = 0.999$ ✓ CC_{word}-$C_{pseudoword}$: $p < 0.001$
2.b C-C pairs: Correct answer more likely in AOI group than AI group	✓ $p = 0.005$

The final spelling task (2c in Figure 5.6) showed that the AOI group had learned the word spellings with a mean accuracy of 97%. Learners exposed to new words without spelling spelled them about half with a letter and half with a doublet.

Discussion

Results confirmed that gemination in an English$_{L+}$ word is established upon first learning, if the spoken word is accompanied by the word spelling containing a doublet. Upon hearing the same new spoken word, learners who had seen a doublet-spelling consistently learnt the word with a geminate, as reflected by a ratio of around 1.5 and rhyme judgment accuracy of less than 70% in $CC_{pseudoword}$-C_{word} and CC_{word}-$C_{pseudoword}$ pairs. Pairs where both lexical items were spelled with a letter yielded a ratio of around one and accuracy above 90%. This shows that the same spoken word can be learned as containing a geminate or a singleton exclusively based on orthographic input, even while repeatedly listening production to a native speaker's production. Single-letter spelling also helps learners establish a word representation containing a singleton consonant, compared with peers who were only exposed to auditory input.

While other experimental studies had also found OEs in the early stages of pseudoword learning, such studies had investigated the learning of actual sounds that were present in the auditory input. The present study established experimentally that orthography results in the learning of a sound that is neither attested in the target phonological system nor present in the auditory input.

Learners who were only exposed to auditory input also learnt some words as containing a geminate. Gemination is probably less frequent in English$_{L+}$ vocabulary learning than in this experiment because the pseudowords used in this study were generated from real English words that can be spelled with a doublet in English, where gemination is legal in Italian, and where Italians produce geminates.

Results also confirmed the link between speech production, awareness, and spelling (see Question 6). Those who spelled a new word with a doublet tended to pronounce it with a geminate, and those who spelled it with a letter tended to pronounce it with a singleton, as shown by Sokolović-Perović et al. (2020) with real words. This supports the view that phonological and orthographic production reflect the same phonological representation. It appears that orthography affects L+ phonological representations from the very early stages of word learning.

Question 8: Does learning that English has no contrastive consonant length reduce the production and categorisation of English$_{L+}$ consonants as geminates?

No. Teaching experienced Italian$_{L1}$ learners of English$_{L+}$ that English doublets do not represent geminates does not stop them from either producing geminates or categorising English consonants as geminates, as geminate:singleton ratios and acceptance of C-CC rhymes did not differ before and after the teaching intervention.

Having shown that naturalistic exposure alone does not reduce OEs on L+ phonology, the next question was: Could instruction be effective? Explicit phonetic instruction can improve L0 and L+ perception and production even for difficult sounds and phonological contrasts (see Chapter 2), and the absence of gemination is a simple concept to learn. Furthermore, training helps with contrastive consonant length, improving perception (Sadakata & McQueen, 2013; Sonu et al., 2013) and production (Motohashi Saigo & Hardison, 2009) in an L+, and even in an L0 (Hisagi & Strange, 2011; Porretta & Tucker, 2015). Hence, teaching learners that English consonant length is not contrastive and that orthographic forms are misleading could help them from their production, or at least awareness.

To address this question, students were taught that doublets do not represent geminates in English (Bassetti et al., 2022). Table 5.13 illustrates the design. There were two groups: The GPC group learned that doublets do not

Table 5.13 Design, Bassetti et al. (2022).

Exp.	Methods			Design	
	Participants	Materials	Task	IV	DV
1	87 learners: 42 GPC instruction, 45 Passive Exposure (PE)	20 CC-C pairs	Delayed word repetition	Group (between: GPC, PE)*Time of testing (within: Pre-, post-test)	CC:C ratio
2	88 learners: 43 GPC, 45 PE	12 CC-C pairs, 24 controls	Rhyme judgment	Group (between: GPC, PE) *Time of testing (within: Pre-, post-test) *Type of pair (within: C-CC, controls)	Accuracy (correct, incorrect)

represent geminates; the passive exposure group practised the same words with no mention of doublets or gemination (see Figure 3.3 for a discussion of participant recruitment and numbers).

A simple and short teaching session was devised and administered to a group of instructed learners. The teaching session required little time (half an hour) and few resources (handouts, projector, and loudspeakers), so that, if successful, it could be adopted by English language teachers. Effects on consonant production and categorisation were tested by comparing pre-instruction and post-instruction performance in the instructed group and a control group. While usually phonetic instruction studies investigate effects on pronunciation, the present study also tested effects on awareness because effects may be more evident in a less demanding task — an untimed judgment task— than in a speech production task where time pressures and demands on mental resources reduce participants' ability to focus on forms.

The sessions were delivered by the present author to each of the eight classes attended by participants. As shown in Figure 3.3, the classes were paired (same teacher or same school), and within each pair, one class was randomly allocated to the GPC instruction and the other to the control (Passive Exposure) instruction. All participants were tested twice, before and after the teaching session, with the same tasks and words.

Figure 5.7 illustrates the GPC instruction session. The 30-minute session simply clarified that doublets do not represent geminates. To maximise its efficacy, it included a variety of activities: Awareness training (student reflection) and explicit teaching, auditory, orthographic input, and pair- and group-work.

84 *Effects of orthography on L+ awareness, perception and learning*

---

1. Awareness training

Whole-class activity:
1a. Hear [ˈfɪnɪʃ], spell it
1b. Listen to two sentences, write the missing words *(finish, Finnish)*

> I don't _____ food I don't like.
> I don't like _____ food.

1c. Discuss whether the two words differ

---

2. Explicit teaching

Mini-lecture on 'Double letters in English orthography and pronunciation'

---

3. Practice

3a. Produce-listen-repeat; researcher-led whole-class activity,
   40 CC-words (3- to 20-letter long):
   - Read a word aloud
   - Listen to word recording, noticing pronunciation
   - Repeat word aloud

3b. Pronunciation-feedback: pair work; one student reads aloud a C-CC word, the other student feedbacks on pronunciation, x 10 words per student

12-16 letters	17-20 letters
Differential	Telecommunication
Collaborator	Interrelationship
Unacceptable	Commercialization
Approximately	Immunohistochemistry
Symmetrically	
Disappointing	happy
Impressionable	
Uncontrollably	
Microprocessor	
Extracurricular	
Immunodeficiency	
Extraterrestrial	/hæpi/

---

4. Consolidation

4a. Homophone-matching:
   worksheet-based pair-work: strike-through 11 pairs
   of C-CC homophones *(analyst-annalist)* from a word cloud

4b. Pronounce-listen-repeat:
   whole-class activity, same task as 3a,
   same 11 words as 4a.

> rebilled moused
> posesed annalist
> balled loot owed tea rebuild
> bale beatles ode dear
> means hool bout matte
> cheap cannon ass vein jute
> past titled ass all cannon mode
> tut hed aut chilly ceto too
> hoos loud ball chili bout
> analyst beatles priest
> bald meet t cheep
> tel pressed duer
> hose assent
> two

Figure 5.7 The GPC instruction.

For the Passive Exposure group — the control group — the session covered derivation and word formation, including awareness training (about derived word structure), explicit teaching (morphemes and suffixes), practice (word-decomposition and word-building), and consolidation (pronounce-listen-repeat task).

To ensure that group differences could only be attributed to the instruction, both groups practised the same words for the same amount of time, with similar mixtures of spoken and written input and types of activities, and with the same teacher (the author). Students were not told that this guest-teacher session was part of the research project or that different classes would learn different things. Finally, words used for testing were not included in the teaching session.

Instruction did not affect either consonant production or categorisation. As the top row in Table 5.14 shows, CC-consonants were about 1.5 times as long as C-consonants both before and after the instruction sessions in both groups. The final model, $RATIO\_LOG \sim TIME\_OF\_TESTING + (1|PARTICIPANT) +$

Table 5.14 Predictions and results, Bassetti et al. (2022).

Exp.	Predictions	Results
1	GPC group only: Lower CC:C ratio after the teaching session than before	✗ No group differences. The ratio decreased slightly in both groups, from 1.54 [1.51;1.58] to 1.49 [1.46;1.53], $p = 0.018$
2	GPC group only: Correct responses to CC-C rhymes are more likely after the session than before	✗ No pre-/post-test differences for either group (pre: 59% [56;62]; post: 58% [55;61]): $p = 0.932$.

(1|WORDPAIR), revealed that CC:C ratios were slightly lower in the second test than in the first test in both groups, regardless of the instruction received, but the ratio was still around 1.5.

The percentage of correct answers in the rhyme judgment task (second row, Table 5.14) was almost identical in the pre- and post-tests in both groups. The final model, *ACCURACY ~ LEARNING_GROUP * TIME_OF_TESTING * PAIR_TYPE + (PAIR_TYPE|PARTICIPANT) + (1|WORDPAIR)*, and post-hoc tests revealed that the likelihood of accuracy for C-CC rhymes did not increase after the instruction in either group ($p = 0.932$), whereas both groups improved with control pairs ($p = 0.001$).

Discussion

Learning that English doublets do not represent geminates did not eliminate or reduce the production or categorisation of English consonants as geminates in experienced L+ learners. The group that had been trained in grapheme-phoneme conversion rules produced consonants with similar geminate:singleton ratios (around 1.5) and had a similar likelihood of rejecting singleton-geminate rhymes before and after the instruction.

This was the first experimental study of a teaching intervention tackling OEs in an L+. Results were in line with previous studies that found no results of instruction in L0s, which are, however, not necessarily representative of actual L+ learning, as discussed.

However, it is too early to conclude that instruction is ineffective, and future researchers could try different materials, methods, or tasks. Above all, considering that phonetic training seems more successful with beginners (Lee et al., 2020), future interventions may target beginner learners.

L+ awareness, speech perception, and learning: A summary of findings

The studies reported earlier show that Italian$_{L1}$ speakers make a contrast between singleton and geminate consonants in English$_{L+}$ that affects their phonological awareness, speech sound perception, and vocabulary acquisition. Italians perceive the same consonant in the same spoken word as a singleton if the word is spelled with a letter and as a geminate if the word is spelled with a doublet, for instance, perceiving different sounds in the homophones *finish* and *Finnish*. In awareness tasks, Italians consider the same consonant as two different consonants in two words where it is spelled with a letter and with a doublet, respectively, such as *very* and *merry*, therefore thinking that such word pairs are not rhymes. Italian learners of English learn that a new spoken English word contains a geminate if they see the word's spelling that contains a doublet, but not if they see the same word spelled with a letter or with no orthographic input. Finally, teaching Italian learners that doublets do not represent geminates have no impact on their awareness or production, as they continue to classify and produce English consonants as geminates.

All the studies reported in Chapters 4 and 5 converge in showing that Italians make a contrast in their English$_{L+}$ phonological systems that is not attested in the phonological systems of English natives and that is caused by orthographic input. This contrast is reflected in Italians' English$_{L+}$ speech perception, speech production, phonological awareness, and vocabulary learning. The final chapter discusses the meaning and implications of these findings.

References

Bassetti, B., Mairano, P., Masterson, J., & Cerni, T. (2020). Effects of orthographic forms on phonological awareness and speech production in second language speakers, with consideration of speaker variables. *Language Learning, 70*(4), *1218–1256*. doi:10.1111/lang.12423

Bassetti, B., Masterson, J., Cerni, T., & Mairano, P. (2021). Orthographic forms affect speech perception in a second language: Consonant and vowel length in L2 English. *Journal of Experimental Psychology: Human Perception and Performance, 47*, 1583–1603. doi:10.1037/xhp0000949

Bassetti, B., et al. (2022). The efficacy of grapheme-phoneme correspondence instruction in reducing the effect of orthographic forms on second language phonology. *Applied Psycholinguistics, 43*(3), 683–705.

Cerni, T., et al. (2019). Effects of orthographic forms on the acquisition of novel spoken words in a second language. *Frontiers in Communication, 4*(31). https://doi.org/10.3389/fcomm.2019.00031

Hisagi, M., & Strange, W. (2011). Perception of Japanese temporally-cued contrasts by American English listeners. *Language and Speech, 54*, 241–264. https://doi.org/10.1177/0023830910397499

Lee, B., et al. (2020). The effects of perception-vs. production-based pronunciation instruction. *System, 88*, 102185. https://doi.org/10.1016/j.system.2019.102185

Motohashi Saigo, M., & Hardison, D. M. (2009). Acquisition of L2 Japanese geminates: Training with waveform displays. *Language Learning & Technology, 13*(2), 29–47. http://dx.doi.org/10125/44179

Porretta, V. J., & Tucker, B. V. (2015). Perception of non-native consonant length contrast: The role of attention in phonetic processing. *Second Language Research, 31*(2), 239–265. https://doi.org/10.1177/0267658314559573

Sadakata, M., & McQueen, J. M. (2013). High stimulus variability in nonnative speech learning supports formation of abstract categories: Evidence from Japanese geminates. *Journal of the Acoustical Society of America, 134*(2), 1324–1335. https://doi.org/10.1121/1.4812767

Simonchyk, A., & Darcy, I. (2018). The effect of orthography on the lexical encoding of palatalized consonants in L2 Russian. *Language and Speech, 61*(4), 522–546. https://doi.org/10.1177/0023830918761490

Sokolović-Perović, M., Bassetti, B., Dillon, S. (2020) English orthographic forms affect L2 English speech production in native users of a non-alphabetic writing system. *Bilingualism: Language and Cognition, 23*(3), 591–601. https://doi.org/10.1017/S136672891900035X

Sonu, M., et al. (2013). Non-native perception and learning of the phonemic length contrast in spoken Japanese: Training Korean listeners using words with geminate and singleton phonemes. *Journal of East Asian Linguistics, 22*(4), 373–398. https://doi.org/10.1007/s10831-013-9107-1

Veivo, O., et al. (2016). Orthographic activation in L2 spoken word recognition depends on proficiency: Evidence from eye-tracking. *Frontiers in Psychology, 7*, 1120. https://doi.org/10.3389/fpsyg.2016.01120

6 Characteristics, causes, and implications of orthographic effects on L+ phonology

Chapter 6 discusses the findings of the project, their significance, and their implications. After summarising the project's findings, this chapter discusses what such findings tell us about orthography, phonology, and their interaction, and how orthographic and auditory input contribute to establishing and reinforcing L+ phonological forms. Finally, implications are discussed for theory (linguistic relativism, bilingual cognition, L+ phonology, and cognitive psychology), research methodology, and language teaching practice.

Summary and significance of findings

Summary of findings

The project's main finding is that orthography can lead plus-language (L+) speakers to make a phonological contrast that is not attested in the phonological system of the target language. This affects L+ learners' and users' L+ phonological systems — which feature a contrast that is unattested in the phonological systems of native speakers of the target language — and phonological lexicons — which feature mental representations of words containing a sound that is not attested in the target language.

Results show that Italian native speakers of English as a plus language ($English_{L+}$) make a contrast between a singleton consonant category and a geminate consonant category in their $English_{L+}$ phonological systems. This singleton-geminate phonological contrast is unattested in native Standard English. It corresponds to the letter-doublet (double letters) orthographic contrast in the English orthographic system, connected by <C>-/C/ and <CC>-/C:/ grapheme-phoneme correspondences, whereby a consonant letter represents a singleton and a consonant doublet represents a geminate.

Italians' $English_{L+}$ phonological system therefore has two phonological categories that correspond to the same phonological category in native speakers' phonological systems. This is not simply a phonetic longer duration of a consonant, it is actually contrastive, as shown by the existence of minimal

DOI: 10.4324/9780429343117-6

pairs in perception and production. What are phonetic variants in the native speaker's mind actually contrast lexical items in the Italian$_{L1}$-English$_{L+}$ speaker's mind.

This phonological contrast affects Italians' English$_{L+}$ representation and processing. (1) Looking at representation, Italians' mental lexicons feature English$_{L+}$ phonological words that contain a geminate. This happens because Italians phonologically recode the orthographic forms of English consonants as a singleton if the consonant is spelled with a letter or as a geminate if it is spelled with a doublet. This can even result in homophones being perceived and produced as a minimal pair (two different spoken words, one containing a singleton and one containing a geminate), if the homophones are spelled with a single letter versus a doublet. This contrast is lexically encoded, meaning that it is encoded at the level of single words, depending on their spelling. (2) Looking at processing, consonant gemination was consistently found in Italians' speech production, speech perception, awareness, and learning, and it persisted in spite of lengthy naturalistic exposure and even a teaching intervention.

To summarise, English$_{L+}$ gemination happens because:

- the English writing system has allographs, as the same consonant can be represented with a single consonant letter <C> or double consonant letters (doublet) <CC>
- the Italian phonological system contrasts singleton consonants /C/ and geminate consonants /C:/
- the Italian writing system represents singletons with a single consonant letter (<C>=/C/) and geminates with a consonant doublet (<CC>=/C:/).

This results in a discrepancy between English GPCs and Italians' English$_{L+}$ orthographic knowledge. This discrepancy has a number of consequences:

- Italians' English$_{L+}$ phonological systems (their mental representations of English phonology) contain length as a feature of consonants, contrasting consonant pairs such as /n/ and /n:/
- Italians' English$_{L+}$ orthographic knowledge includes a <CC>=/C:/ grapheme-phoneme conversion rule, whereby a consonant doublet represents a geminate consonant
- Italians' English$_{L+}$ mental lexicons contain English$_{L+}$ word representations that feature a geminate, such as ['fɪn:ɪʃ]
- if the mental representation of an English$_{L+}$ word contains a geminate, this affects all aspects of that word's processing so that the consonant is perceived, produced, and categorised as a geminate.

The next section lists the project's findings with regards to each of the research questions presented in Chapter 3.

Research questions and related findings

Table 6.1 shows the outcome for each of the research questions listed in Table 3.1. In summary, Italian$_{L1}$ speakers produce singleton and geminate consonants in English$_{L+}$, depending on consonant spelling, namely single letter or double letters (Question 1). However, their English$_{L+}$ geminates are about 1.5 times as long as the corresponding singletons, that is to say, shorter than their Italian$_{L1}$ geminates, which are about twice as long as the corresponding singleton. Italians' English$_{L+}$ gemination is lexically contrastive (Question 2), as they produce minimal pairs that are distinguished only by the duration of a consonant, and there is no overlap in the durations of their singleton consonants and corresponding geminates. There appear to be predictors of gemination in Italian$_{L1}$ speakers' English$_{L+}$ speech production (Question 3); in particular, higher English$_{L+}$ proficiency seems associated with lower degrees of gemination, and an L1 geminated cognate seems associated with higher degrees of gemination in English words. However, the results were not neat, and more research is needed. In particular, the effects of naturalistic exposure were unclear, as differences between instructed learners and UK-based late bilinguals were inconsistent. Italian$_{L1}$ speakers categorise the same English$_{L+}$ consonant as singleton or geminate depending on its spelling (Question 4), as they reject rhymes where the same consonant is spelled with a single letter or a doublet, such as *very-merry*, and explain that the two words contain different

Table 6.1 Project's research questions and findings.

Aspect of phonology	Research Question	Findings
Production	**Q1.** Do Italian$_{L1}$ speakers produce singleton and geminate consonants in English$_{L+}$, depending on consonant spelling?	✓
	Q2. Is Italian$_{L1}$ speakers' English$_{L+}$ gemination lexically contrastive?	✓
	Q3. Are there predictors of gemination in Italian$_{L1}$ speakers' English$_{L+}$ speech production?	✓
Awareness	**Q4.** Do Italian$_{L1}$ speakers categorise the same English$_{L+}$ consonant as singleton versus geminate, depending on its spelling?	✓
Perception	**Q5.** Do Italian$_{L1}$ speakers perceive the same English$_{L+}$ consonant as singleton or geminate, depending on its spelling?	✓
All	**Q6.** Is there a correlation between perception, production, and categorisation of geminates in English$_{L+}$?	✓
Learning:	**Q7.** Lexical learning: Do Italian$_{L1}$ speakers learn new spoken English words as containing a geminate if they learn them with a double-letter spelling?	✓
	Q8. Phonological learning: Does learning that English has no contrastive consonant length reduce Italians' production and categorisation of geminates?	✗

consonants because one is long. Italian$_{L1}$ speakers also perceive the same English$_{L+}$ consonant as singleton or geminate, depending on its spelling (Question 5), as they believe they perceive different sounds in homophones such as *finish-Finnish*. Interestingly, there appears to be a correlation between perception, production, and categorisation of geminates (Question 6), meaning that English$_{L+}$ speakers show similar levels of gemination across different L+ phonological processes. Looking at lexical learning, Italian$_{L1}$ learners of English$_{L+}$ learn new spoken English words as containing a geminate if exposed to words spelled with a doublet (Question 7), and just a few exposures are sufficient. Only one prediction was not supported by results: Learning that English has no contrastive consonant length does not reduce Italians' production and categorisation of geminates (Question 8). However, more research is needed before ruling out the possibility that teaching can reduce orthography-induced gemination.

Significance of findings

Two aspects of this project's findings constitute new contributions to the field of OEs on L+ phonology. Findings provide the first experimental evidence of an L+ phonological contrast that is not attested in the target language, and the first systematic empirical evidence that the same OE affects all aspects of L+ phonology. Finally, this was the first evidence that participants' views, elicited through qualitative methods, can confirm and explain OEs.

An unattested phonological contrast. This was the first study to investigate and demonstrate experimentally a phonological contrast in the phonological systems of L+ speakers that is not attested in the phonological systems of native speakers. This is novel because L+ phonology research investigates the acquisition and processing of the phonological contrasts of the target language, not of phonological contrasts that are not attested in the target language.

Prior to this project, the available evidence was limited to anecdotal evidence and non-experimental studies of beginners. These do not constitute evidence of an L+ phonological contrast. An unpublished report of a descriptive study of English$_{L+}$ pronunciation errors in a small group of Italian first-year primary-school children remarked that children read aloud the word *apple* with a long [p] (Browning, 2004). This was one word for early beginners with minimal exposure to the target languages. A study of the production of stop consonants in Spanish$_{L+}$ beginners (Zampini, 1994) found frequent substitutions of [b] with [v] in words spelled with <v>, although in Spanish [v] is not attested as either a phoneme or allophone and <v> is an allograph of <b>. This was not an experiment, and this substitution may simply reflect an early stage in L+ phonological development, as it was more frequent among first- than second-year students and in reading aloud than in conversation, and was also later demonstrated experimentally in naïve listeners upon first exposure to Spanish (Rafat, 2016). This project then provided both the first experimental evidence and the first evidence from experienced L+ speakers, showing experimentally that orthography can lead L+ speakers beyond the very early stages to make a categorical distinction between two L+ sounds that belong to the same category to a native speaker.

A pervasive OE. The project provides the first systematic empirical evidence that the same OE is found across all aspects of L+ phonology — perception, production, awareness, and learning. Consonant doublets in orthographic words result in the illusory perception of geminates in speech perception, the production of geminates and singletons in reading-aloud and in speech production, the categorisation of the same consonant as a geminate or singleton in awareness tasks, and the learning of new words as containing a geminate. Previous OE studies mostly focused on production, perception, or occasionally awareness, with various studies of lexical learning. The same OE was sometimes studied more than once in replications or extensions of previous research, but there was not a single study that investigated the same OE across all phonological processes.

The importance of participants' views. Finally, this was the first study to elicit participants' views to confirm and explain an OE. Previous experimental research had never asked participants their thoughts about the OE. Rather than assuming that participants were perceiving and producing geminates, this study elicited their views. Participants' views indeed confirmed the researchers' interpretation of their experimental findings. It is then to be hoped that future research will include this type of qualitative data.

Confirming and extending previous research on OEs

This section discusses the characteristics and peculiarities of orthography-induced gemination vis-a-vis other previously reported OEs, while the next section looks at previous research on L+ phonology. $English_{L+}$ gemination aligns with other OEs in that it falls under the category of L1-influenced unattested GPCs, and it meets Bassetti's (2008, 2024) criteria for identifying OEs, confirming both the orthographic nature of $English_{L+}$ gemination and the validity of Bassetti's criteria. Yet, $English_{L+}$ gemination also differs from previously reported OEs, crucially because it results in a L+ phonological category that is not attested in the target language, but also because it affects a whole class of consonants and the outcome sounds are in-between the L1 and L+ sounds. Finally, the section discusses studies by other scholars that found the same OE in native speakers of different L1s, confirming the present findings.

$English_{L+}$ gemination is a sound substitution caused by an L1-induced unattested GPC

Looking at the classification of OEs in Chapter 2, L+ gemination can be classified as a sound substitution. For instance, [nː] is substituted for [n]. This is not an unusual finding, as substitutions are the most frequently reported OEs in the literature.

The cause of English$_{L+}$ gemination is an *L1-influenced unattested GPC* (see Chapter 2). It is unattested because this GPC is not present in native speakers' orthographic knowledge, as English natives do not recode doublets as geminates. It is L1-influenced because — as is often the case with this type of GPCs — it originates from an incongruence between the GPCs of the L1 and the L+. This L1-L+ incongruence results in a difference between the GPCs of the English writing system on the one hand and the orthographic knowledge in the minds of Italian$_{L1}$-English$_{L+}$ speakers. In English, single letter <C> and doublet <CC> are homographs — different written forms of the same phoneme /C/. However, Italians' English$_{L+}$ phonological system has two phonological categories that correspond to the same phonological category in native speakers' phonological systems.

English$_{L+}$ gemination is an OE

Gemination in English$_{L+}$ meets all of the criteria proposed by Bassetti (2008, 2024) to determine the orthographic nature of an L+ phonological phenomenon. As a general principle, an OE should have an orthographic explanation and should not be explainable in terms of phonology alone. English$_{L+}$ gemination meets all the criteria as follows:

1) *Attributable to orthography.* English$_{L+}$ gemination can be explained by orthography because in Italian$_{L1}$ a consonant doublet represents a geminate.
2) *Not solely attributable to L1 phonology or the L1 phonological lexicon.* L1 lexical gemination is a necessary condition — obviously if there was no gemination in the L1, there would not be gemination in the L+ — but is not a sufficient condition. English$_{L+}$ gemination cannot be explained solely by the following:

   (2a) Italian phonology (phonological categories, phonological contrasts, or phonotactic rules). As evidence, singletons can occur in the same contexts where geminates are produced (for instance, both [n] and [n:] are possible in [fi_iʃ]), Italian$_{L1}$ speakers who acquired English$_{L+}$ early and naturalistically do not geminate in correspondence of doublet spellings (Repetti, 2009), and Italians tend not to geminate in new spoken English$_{L+}$ words they have learnt without exposure to orthographic forms

   (2b) the phonological form of L1 cognates. As evidence, gemination is found in English$_{L+}$ CC-words with no Italian$_{L1}$ cognate (*kitty*) or with a cognate that contains a singleton, such as *pepper*, in Italian *pepe*. An Italian$_{L1}$ geminated cognate is not necessary for gemination to occur (if anything, it may make gemination stronger, but the evidence is not conclusive).

3) *Not solely attributable to other phonological factors*: The phonology of the L+, its acquisition, or universals of phonological development:

    3a) L+ phonology. Contrastive length is not attested in English$_{L1}$ speech (for a detailed discussion, see 'Consonant length in English' in Chapter 3).

    3b) characteristics of phonological development. Gemination is not attested in English$_{L1}$ infants' language acquisition (or indeed Italian-English early bilinguals)

    3c) universals of phonological acquisition. Gemination is marked — relatively rare among world languages (it featured in less than 4% of the languages surveyed by Maddieson, 1984) — hence unlikely to emerge in phonological development.

English$_{L+}$ gemination is a peculiar OE

Orthography-induced gemination is also peculiar within the OE literature. First, the outcome is the substitution of an L+ sound with a sound that is not attested in the L+ phonological system of the language. Second, the sound that is produced is in-between an L1 and an L+ sound. Finally, the cause is not a single GPC but the correspondence between an orthographic feature and a phonological feature, which results in various unattested GPCs.

The outcome contrast is not attested in native phonological systems. Unlike all previous findings in the literature, the present OE results in a contrast that is not attested in English natives' perception, production, and awareness (see 'Significance of Findings' presented earlier). So far, research has documented sound substitutions whereby a target sound is replaced with another L+ sound — [d] for [t], [b] for [β] — or L+ allophone — [t] for [ɾ] (see Chapter 2). As Figure 4.3 shows, English native speakers did not produce either a singleton-geminate contrast or consonants as long as Italians' English$_{L+}$ geminates. The sound produced by Italians is not an English sound or allophone, but a sound that is not attested in native speakers' production, where such long consonants were not found. These long consonants are different sounds only in the phonological system of Italian-English speakers and in the Italian variety of English (see 'The phonological inventory of Italian English' presented later).

The outcome sound is in-between an L1 and an L+ sound. The outcome sound is unattested not only in English speech, but also in native Italians' speech, as Italians realise English$_{L+}$ geminates with half of the durational difference between Italian singleton and geminate consonants (Bassetti et al., 2018). This project found a mean CC:C ratio of 1.33 in bilinguals and 1.55 in learners (see Chapter 4), whereas geminates are twice as long as their singleton counterparts in the participants' native variety of Roman Italian (Esposito & Di Benedetto, 1999). Indeed, Bassetti and colleagues (2018) directly compared participants' production of intervocalic geminates in Italian$_{L1}$ and English$_{L+}$ and found that geminates were more than twice as long as corresponding singletons in Italian$_{L1}$ (mean CC:C ratio = 2.47), but only about 1.4 times as long as singletons in English$_{L+}$. The duration of Italians' English$_{L+}$ geminates is then in-between the durations of L1 geminates and L+ consonants.

The cause is not a single GPC. Orthography-induced gemination does not happen at the level of a grapheme-phoneme correspondence but at the level of orthographic and phonological features, which affect a whole class of GPCs, as Italians establish a correspondence between the orthographic feature [±double] in their English$_{L+}$ orthographic knowledge and the [±long] feature in their English$_{L+}$ phonological systems. This is a special case of L1-L+ orthographic incongruence, as the incongruent written representation of length, where doublets represent gemination in the L1 but not in the L+, affects a whole set of consonants. This is a rare finding in the literature; only Barrios and Hayes-Harb (2020) looked above the level of GPCs, as they argued that orthography-induced voicing of word-final stops in German$_{L0}$ is an effect of orthography on a phonological process rather than a phonological category. The present findings show the effects of orthography on a class of consonants rather than a single phoneme.

Further evidence: Beyond Italian$_{L1}$-English$_{L+}$ speakers

Finally, it should be noticed that this project's first findings led to a number of studies by other researchers that investigated — and confirmed — orthography-induced L+ gemination. These results show that orthography-induced gemination is not limited to L+ English but also appears in L+ French, and it is found in L1 speakers of some languages other than Italian.

The first two studies, which both appeared in 2018, were led by two postdoctoral fellows on this project. Sokolović-Perović, in collaboration with the present author and a graduate student (Sokolović-Perović et al., 2020), used the same task as Bassetti (2017) and found gemination in the consonant production of Japanese$_{L1}$-English$_{L+}$ speakers living in the United Kingdom. In the same year, a conference presentation by Mairano and colleagues (Mairano et al., 2018b) found gemination in Italian$_{L1}$ university students of French, another language that has no lexical gemination.

Orthography-induced gemination was then also found in Jordanian Arabic$_{L1}$ speakers of French$_{L+}$ (Nawafleh, 2022) and in Korean$_{L1}$ but not in Farsi$_{L1}$ speakers of English$_{L+}$, possibly because Farsi has a less transparent writing system (Rafat et al., 2021). Finally, Mitterer (2021) found no evidence of gemination in Maltese$_{L1}$-English$_{L+}$ early bilinguals using Bassetti's (2017) task, probably because early bilinguals are not influenced by orthography.

These studies only investigated production, so this project's evidence from perception, awareness, and learning will need to be replicated. An interesting exception is Nawafleh (2022), who also investigated perception and found that Arabic$_{L1}$ listeners indeed perceive English$_{L+}$ geminates produced by fellow Arabic$_{L1}$ speakers as geminates, although this may be due to the effects of orthography on their perception rather than the actual duration of the consonants they heard. Overall, these findings suggest that orthography-induced L+ gemination is widespread beyond the Italian$_{L1}$-English$_{L+}$ population.

Extending previous research on L+ phonology

The consonant length contrast in English$_{L+}$ is a peculiar phenomenon within the L+ phonology literature, as it is a rare case of a two-to-one category scenario. Furthermore, it is persistent in spite of being arguably not particularly difficult to acquire, and it arguably results in differences between the phonological inventories of Standard English and Italian English.

The two-to-one category scenario

The project revealed a scenario that has not received attention in L+ phonology research: The L1 has two phonological categories that align with one category in the L+. Both theory and empirical research so far focussed on L+ phonological contrasts that align to one category in learners' L1.

The typical scenario — where the L1 has one category corresponding to singleton and geminate in the L+ — causes difficulty in both learning and processing L+ consonant length contrasts, which L+ listeners cannot perceive. This is well established across languages, including Italian$_{L+}$ (De Clercq et al., 2014; Sorianello, 2014). In this scenario, L+ learners have difficulty perceiving durational differences, tend to have fuzzy rather than categorical boundaries, and when they do have categorical boundaries, these do not coincide with natives' boundaries.

This study reveals the opposite: It is not the presence but the absence of durational contrasts that is hard to perceive. It appears that it is difficult to ignore or unlearn an L1 phonological contrast that is not attested in the L+, both among learners and experienced users. Implications for models of L+ phonological development are discussed later. At any rate, these results are novel in that they reverse the usual approach to L+ phonology research.

The persistence of orthography-induced gemination

Given that training usually has a positive impact on L+ phonology, the lack of effects of this project's intervention may indicate that OEs are more resistant to change than other factors — such as the effects of L1 phonology — that are not reinforced by orthographic input. This is an unknown, given that no other study has investigated the impact of training on L+ OEs.

The intervention reversed the usual approach to L+ training. Interventions usually train L+ speakers to notice differences they learned to ignore in the process of L1 phonological acquisition, which are needed to discriminate L+ sounds. Conversely, this project's intervention trained L+ speakers to unlearn to discriminate, ignoring a difference that is relevant to L1 but not L+ phonology.

Training has positive effects on L+ consonant length contrasts in the usual one-to-two scenario (no length contrast in the L1, two length categories in the L+), for instance in Japanese$_{L+}$ (Sadakata & McQueen, 2013), but does not impact this arguably easier two-to-one scenario. Various explanations are possible, including perhaps issues with the design or implementation of the intervention, but it is also possible that orthography-reinforced effects are more resistant to change than purely linguistic effects. This point was made by Mairano and colleagues (2018a) in their comparison of VOT and gemination in Italians' English$_{L+}$ production. To address this issue, future research should further test the effects of teaching, possibly comparing its effects on similar L+ phenomena, only one of which is caused by orthography.

The phonological inventory of Italian English

In light of these findings, linguistic descriptions of the phonological repertoire of Italian English should then include the feature of consonant length. If one embraces the view that phonological repertoires should include separate phonological categories for singletons and their corresponding geminates, then the Italian variety of English would have a much larger number of consonant categories compared with standard varieties of English.

This consonant length contrast is only found in the Italian variety of English used in Italy, not in the English of Italian emigrant communities in English-speaking countries. Repetti (2009) found no orthography-induced gemination in the Italian community in Canada, whose gemination was non-lexical, caused by phonological processes, and unrelated to consonant spelling.

Explaining orthography-induced gemination: The orthography-phonology interface

This section argues that there may be sources of reinforcing evidence other than orthographic input that may explain the persistence of orthography-induced English$_{L+}$ gemination in Italian speakers, despite the lack of durational differences in targetlike spoken input. The proposed sources include (1) targetlike input (produced by L1 or L+ speakers), (2) non-targetlike input, and (3) other sources. Specifically, reinforcing evidence may include (1a) the strategic ignoring of targetlike spoken percepts, (1b) the misperception of spoken input due to orthography, (1c) the presence of non-contrastive gemination in targetlike speech, (1d) the absence of negative evidence, (2a) gemination in non-targetlike input produced by native speakers of Italian or other geminated languages, (2b) gemination in the L+ speaker's own output, and (3) sources other than English language input. The proposed sources of evidence are not mutually exclusive, and more than one may be at play. A more detailed discussion follows.

1a. Strategically ignored targetlike spoken input Italian$_{L1}$ listeners may overextend a successful strategy for L+ listening, namely relying on orthography and ignoring their own percepts. This strategy is successfully employed by L+ listeners who cannot perceive a phonological contrast. For instance, English$_{L+}$ listeners who cannot discriminate between two English vowels can ignore their perceived similarity and rely on vowel spellings to identify the correct vowel (Escudero et al., 2008), as indeed Italian$_{L1}$-English$_{L+}$ listeners do (Piske et al., 2002; Bassetti et al., 2018, 2020). Italian$_{L+}$ listeners who cannot perceive Italian$_{L+}$ consonant length contrasts can ignore the perceived similarity and rely on consonant spelling to distinguish geminates and singletons. Italian$_{L1}$-English$_{L+}$ listeners, who cannot perceive a durational difference in English$_{L+}$ consonants because there is not one, may erroneously adopt the same strategy.

1b. Corroborating evidence: Orthography-influenced intake L+ listeners' phonological intake may provide evidence of gemination even though it is not present in their input, due to orthography-induced misperception of the spoken input.

Italians illusorily perceive geminates in English native input because of top-down influences caused by the orthographic form of words, for instance, perceiving [fɪnɪʃ] as [fɪn:ɪʃ]. Hence, a geminate that is not present in the spoken input may be present in the L+ listener's intake.

1c. Corroborating evidence: Non-contrastive gemination in targetlike speech. Italians may erroneously attribute a phonological status to the false gemination present in native or non-native targetlike English speech (longer consonants at morpheme boundaries in compounds and derived words such as *top pick, unnamed*; see 'Consonant length in English' in Chapter 3). Italians may, for instance, consider the shorter and longer [p] in *topic-top pick* as evidence of lexical gemination.

1d. Corroborating evidence: Lack of negative evidence. Lack of negative evidence can also constitute corroborating evidence. Unlike vowel duration, gemination does not result in either communication disruptions or feedback from interlocutors. If Italians produce a long vowel in *ship*, their interlocutor may hear *sheep*, triggering miscommunication, which can result in noticing the gap (between what the speaker wanted to say and what the interlocutor understood) or receiving feedback. However, gemination is unlikely to affect intelligibility because geminates and singletons are allophones for listeners with no L1 contrastive consonant length.

2a. Gemination in non-targetlike input. Gemination may be frequent and salient in non-targetlike input produced by native speakers of Italian and other geminated languages. It is probably frequent for instructed learners who interact with peers or those living in an English-speaking environment who interact with native speakers of geminated languages, including Arabic, Japanese, and Korean. Italian listeners would find it salient because it has a contrastive function, allowing them to differentiate, for instance, *aloud* from *allowed*.

2b. Gemination in own (overt and covert) output. Gemination is also present in the L+ speaker's own output. This constitutes input too and includes overt speech production, inner speech (talking to oneself in one's mind), and silent reading.

3. Other sources of evidence. There may be other sources of indirect evidence of contrastive consonant length, including gemination in English loanwords to Italian, and English vowel duration, which is contrastive to Italians. Clarification of the relationship between loanword phonology and L+ phonology, as well as between vowel and consonant length, is necessary to determine whether these sources provide supportive evidence.

In summary, orthography-induced gemination is evidence of the complex relationship between orthographic and auditory input. While orthography is the main factor causing and reinforcing in gemination in English$_{L+}$, this section speculates that various types of non-orthographic input may also reinforce gemination. This is all speculative but testable.

Implications

This final section discusses the implications of the project's findings for theory, methods, and practice. Looking at theory, the project mostly contributes to theorising in linguistic relativism and bilingual thought but also has implications for models of L+ phonological development and for cognitive psychological research on language representation and processing. Looking at methodology, the project demonstrates the importance of qualitative research in L+ phonology, contributes tasks and materials, and provides indications for future research. Finally, looking at practice, the project shows that language teachers need to be aware of OEs but should not yet draw conclusions for classroom practice.

Theoretical implications

Implications for linguistic relativism and bilingual cognition

Whether the languages we know affect our thinking is one of the most fundamental questions in the study of language and cognition and the question behind all my research, including this project. As stated in Chapter 3, the project was theoretically grounded in linguistic relativism and multicompetence. Results support and expand linguistic relativism research by showing that language affects categorisation. It is argued that the categorisation both of language sounds and of continua provides good evidence of linguistic relativity and that not only spoken but also written language affects thought. Results also support multi-competence, showing that knowledge of more than one language affects thinking about language.

Language as evidence of linguistic relativity. The study supports linguistic relativity because the same perceptual stimulus (a linguistic sound) was categorised differently by English speakers and Italian-English speakers. Effects were found in both explicit categorisation — rhyme judgment and related open questions — and implicit categorisation (the perception task), and arguably the word repetition tasks.

Researchers have been debating whether the effects of language on thinking about language count as evidence of linguistic relativity. While some objected that these are not effects of 'pure' linguistic relativity, there is no obvious difference between categorising linguistic sounds based on their (perceived) duration and categorising colours based on their brightness (perceived luminous intensity), or non-linguistic sounds based on pitch. Indeed, language is possibly the cognitive domain where effects of language are easiest to show and evidence of linguistic relativity is more plentiful (see Bassetti & Filipović, 2022).

Written language as a source of linguistic relativity effects. The effects were due to written rather than spoken language. This shows that linguistic relativity effects can be multi-modal, with the written modality affecting the spoken modality. This study then contributed to a long line of evidence that written language affects diverse aspects of linguistic and non-linguistic cognition, from concepts of phoneme and word to the directionality of time and the recognition of facial emotion (Bassetti & Cook, 2011). While the phonological categories of native languages are based on first language speech perception, and alphabetic literacy only brings them to consciousness, resulting in phonemic awareness (Cook & Bassetti, 2005), the phonological categories of L+s reflect not only L+ speech perception but also L1 perception and the written representations of the L+.

The categorisation of continua as evidence of linguistic relativity. The study also confirms that the categorisation of continua can provide strong evidence of linguistic relativity. Language often affects the categorisation of a continuum, including the number of categories and categorical boundaries. For instance, speakers of different languages divide the colour spectrum into different colour categories, and have different prototypes and boundaries for their colour categories. Looking at speech sounds, speakers of different languages divide the same acoustic continuum into different categories — such as English /r-l/ versus the Japanese single liquid category — or have different categorical boundaries — for instance, between /b/ and /p/ on the voice onset time continuum. This study indeed shows that Italians divide the English consonant duration continuum into two phonological categories, while English speakers do not.

Linguistic relativism and the multi-competent user of more than one language. Finally, results confirm that bilinguals think differently than monolingual speakers of their two languages, supporting the tenets of multi-competence. Among the four types of bilingual concepts proposed by Bassetti and Cook (2011), English geminates belong to the 'one-integrated-concept' type, that is to say, a concept that falls in-between an L1 and an L2 concept. A typical example is English-Greek bilinguals' concepts of 'blue', which is darker than L2 *blue* and lighter than L1 *blu*. Similarly, the Italian-English speakers' concept of geminate is shorter than an L1 geminate and longer than an English consonant.

In a more traditional approach, Italians' English$_{L+}$ gemination may be considered evidence of cross-language transfer. Yet, this is not transfer because a new, in-between category is created and because this category plays a function in the Italian variety of English, allowing Italians to distinguish minimal pairs in English in speech production (and future research could investigate whether it also facilitates the recognition of English$_{L+}$ words spoken by fellow Italians).

Implications for models of L+ phonological development

Findings raise issues that should be addressed by models of L+ phonological development. It is argued that two models that inspired most empirical research — PAM-L2 and SLM-4 (see Chapter 1) — should consider that orthography affects auditory input, and include the two-to-one phonological category scenario.

SLM-r (Speech Learning Model revised, Flege & Bohn, 2021), which aims at modelling naturalistic L+ speech learning, should consider that orthography is likely to affect naturalistic learners too, for the reasons discussed in 'Explaining orthography-induced gemination: The orthography-phonology interface': Gemination is present in the English$_{L+}$ speech produced by native speakers of geminated languages, and intake can include gemination even when it is not present in the input. Finally, as Young-Scholten and Langer (2015) argued, naturalistic learners may not be exposed to written language in the classroom but are still exposed to environmental written language. Double letters in the linguistic landscape will be recoded as geminates by Italian naturalistic learners of English who are literate in Italian. Hence, SLM-r, which acknowledges the role of accented spoken input in naturalistic exposure, should also include orthography-influenced auditory input and orthographic input.

PAM-L2 (Perceptual Assimilation Model, Best & Tyler, 2007), which aims at modelling the acquisition of L2 contrasts, could add one more pattern of assimilation. The model includes three patterns of assimilation of two L+

contrasting sounds, depending on the number of L1 sounds: Single-category, two-category, and uncategorised (respectively, the L1 has one, two, or no categories corresponding to two L+ contrasting sounds). It could then add a pattern of assimilation whereby the two contrasting sounds are in the L1, and the L+ has only one category, to cover situations where learners establish an L+ phonological contrast that corresponds to two L1 categories and one L+ category, as in the Italians' pattern of assimilation of English$_{L+}$ consonants into two length categories.

Furthermore, when discussing the different patterns of assimilation, the model could also consider the orthographic form of the sounds involved. Best and Tyler (2007) considered spelling as a factor in establishing the equivalence between an L+ and an L1 phonological category, arguing that French$_{L1}$ learners may assimilate English$_{L+}$ voiced alveolar liquid [ɹ] and the very different French$_{L1}$ voiced uvular fricative /ʁ/ to the same phonological category /r/ partly because both are written as <r>. The model could then formally integrate orthographic forms among the sources of input.

Other models and approaches are not discussed here, but similar considerations would apply. In general, L+ phonology scholars should model the effects of orthography on L+ phonological categorisation. In conclusion, orthography-induced gemination, as well as other L2 OEs, can contribute to theorising in L+ phonology.

Implications for language processing research: The locus of OEs

While this project was not intended to address the question of the locus of OEs, a few reflections are possible. Researchers investigating OEs in native speakers have long been debating the issue. Some argued that OEs are caused by the co-activation and conflict between orthographic and phonological representations during speech processing (Ziegler & Ferrand, 1998); others argued that orthographic forms affect phonological representations, and these orthography-influenced phonological representations in turn result in the observed OEs in speech processing (Muneaux & Ziegler, 2004; Taft, 2006). In the case of English$_{L+}$ gemination, the first approach predicts that the English$_{L+}$ speaker co-activates the orthographic representation of *Finnish* and the phonological representation [fɪnɪʃ], and the conflict results in [fɪn:ɪʃ]; the second approach predicts that the written form <Finnish> is recoded as [fɪn:ɪʃ], resulting in the phonological representation [fɪn:ɪʃ], that in turn leads to the production of [fɪn:ɪʃ].

It is argued that L+ OEs are most likely caused by orthography-influenced phonological representations; for instance, orthography-induced English$_{L+}$ gemination is most likely caused by a phonological representation that contains a geminate. This is because L+ speakers are exposed to copious orthographic input in the absence of a mature phonological system or native-like phonological representations, and often learn L+ words mostly — or even exclusively — from written input. As shown in this book, they learn English$_{L+}$ words containing a geminate after very limited exposure to a word spelled with a geminate.

However, the effects of orthography-influenced L+ phonological representations may be compounded by the co-activation of L+ orthographic forms. The CC-word's orthographic representation may be co-activated during speech processing, and its doublet, phonologically recoded using a <CC>=/C:/ correspondence, could reinforce the geminate already present in the phonological representation of the word.

This project cannot contribute to the debate on L1 OEs because it was not designed to test these two proposals and, more importantly, because theories developed to account for L1 OEs should not be assumed to explain L+ OEs, and vice versa. This is because there are huge differences in the nature of OEs between L1 and L+ speakers: There are qualitative differences because some OEs reported in Chapter 2 are only possible in those who know more than one spoken and written language, and quantitative differences because OEs are likely more frequent and stronger in L+ speakers than in L1 speakers, who establish their phonological system and phonological representations well before learning orthography. Future research could compare OEs in L1 and in additional languages to clarify the relationship between the two.

In summary, this project shows that research on OEs on speech sound categorisation can contribute to research on L+ phonology, linguistic relativism, bilingual cognition, and language processing.

Methodological implications

This study aimed at showcasing ways to address at least some of the methodological issues with OE research that have been discussed in the section on 'Characteristics of the Project' in Chapter 3. The study contributed to the advancement of research methodology first of all by being the first to investigate the effects of one orthographic phenomenon on perception, production, awareness, and phonological and lexical learning. It also introduced the use of qualitative data to support and explain experimental evidence for OEs. Finally, it created new tasks and materials for research on L+ phonology.

This was the first study of OEs in L+ phonology to include qualitative data to support and explain experimental results. The present author has argued elsewhere (Bassetti & Filipović, 2022) that qualitative evidence may be useful in confirming linguistic relativity researchers' interpretation of their experimental findings by adding an emic perspective to data collection and analysis.

This study also contributed a useful set of tasks and materials to study L+ phonology in situations where the most widely used tasks cannot be used because the L+ sound under analysis is not attested in the target language. The delayed word repetition task (Bassetti, 2017; Bassetti et al., 2020) will be useful to elicit words when it is not possible to use images (for instance, non-imageable words), and orthographic input should be avoided (as it would impact results). The consonant perception task (Bassetti et al., 2021) will prove useful for testing the perception of sounds that are not present in the spoken input (not only geminates but also, for instance, silent letters). The rhyme judgment task (Bassetti et al., 2020) will be useful for research on phoneme or rhyme awareness. In terms of materials, the word lists created for this project, and particularly the list of orthographic minimal pairs, will be useful for future research on gemination in L+ English but can also be used to research the spelling of doublets. Furthermore, the study validated some of these tasks by showing a correlation between the awareness task and the production task, which is evidence of the validity of both tasks.

The study also shows that studying linguistic phenomena that do not occur in the English language can broaden horizons not only in theorising but also in methodology. Much of the methodological innovation described earlier came into existence because orthography-induced gemination in English had not been studied before. Tasks created to study the discrimination of a phonological contrast were not suitable to study the illusory discrimination of a non-existing contrast; there were no word lists for comparing consonants spelled with a letter or doublet. It is hoped that as OE research explores new phenomena, existing methods will find new applications and new methods will emerge, to respond to the needs caused by investigating new language phenomena.

The study also addressed the previously mentioned (see Chapter 3) needs for sample sizes that provide sufficient power (based on power analysis), an interdisciplinary team with expertise in the various aspects of OE research (phoneticians, psychologists), and a declared theoretical background to provide testable hypotheses and explanations for results (in this case, linguistic relativity and multi-competence).

Limitations and areas for future research

Being an exploratory first study of a phenomenon (orthography-induced gemination), the project suffers from some limitations, which can be addressed in future studies.

Confounds. These are variables that co-occur with the predictor of interest, so it is unclear whether it was the predictor, the confound, or both that indeed caused the effect, or whether the predictor's effects may have been mitigated by the confound. Looking at participants, the effects of naturalistic exposure were investigated by comparing sequential bilinguals living in the United Kingdom with instructed high-school students in Italy, but proficiency and age of onset of acquisition were both confounds because bilinguals had not only naturalistic exposure but, compared with learners, also had higher proficiency — which could have reduced OEs — and later age of onset — which could have strengthened OEs. Also, learners were tested in Italy and bilinguals in the United Kingdom, and gemination may be stronger when participants are tested in an Italian-speaking environment compared with testing the same participant in an English-speaking environment. Looking at the materials, all experiments involved between-item comparisons, meaning that differences between sets of targets and sets of controls could be at least partly due to intrinsic differences between the two sets.

Sample selection. Participants may not be representative of the populations of interest because participation was voluntary, and this self-selected group may differ from the general population of English learners and users, for instance, by having a stronger interest in research or in language or higher self-perceived proficiency. Indeed, learners in the perception study (which required knowledge of some less common words) had better vocabulary knowledge, higher proficiency, and a higher proportion of spoken language input compared with typical high-school fourth-year students. A perception study that does not require this level of vocabulary knowledge may test learners with lower proficiency and reveal stronger OEs. Also, all learners were fourth-year high-school students. Future research should investigate learners with different lengths of study, and in particular, the intervention study may have been more successful with beginner learners. Furthermore, the strong OEs found in this study may be due to Italians' transparent native orthography or perhaps to the traditional approach to English language teaching in Italian schools. Future research should investigate learners/users with other language combinations, including L1s and L+s with different levels of phonological transparency, non-alphabetic writing systems, and different educational backgrounds.

Tasks and materials. Time and money limitations both prevented the use of more expensive technologies such as eye-tracking and limited the amount of triangulation, so that awareness, perception, and minimal pair production were all investigated with just one experiment each. For instance, it would be interesting to investigate minimal pair production without orthographic input and to investigate perception using a shadowing task to establish whether effects appear prelexically. Also, this study adopted almost exclusively an experimental approach, but future research could investigate gemination in real-life communication to establish whether consonant duration is used to disambiguate homophones in everyday conversation and, if so, whether it is used only with Italian$_{L1}$ interlocutors or also with natives. The study used not only objective measures (for instance, for language proficiency), but also a number of self-reported variables, collected by means of ratings in questionnaires; future research could instead use objective measures. Finally, the study's findings generated new research questions that could not be investigated within this project; for instance, future research could investigate the location of the singleton-geminate boundary in Italian English by investigating categorical boundaries in speech perception.

In conclusion, to make this study's results more generalisable, future research should disentangle the effects of confounds, investigate other types of speakers using different methods, and tackle the various new research questions that stemmed from the new evidence produced by this study.

Practical implications for language teaching

No recommendations for language teaching practice can be made based on a single intervention study that yielded null results, but some issues can already be addressed.

First, teachers of languages that are written with the roman alphabet — including English — should be aware that native speakers of languages that have gemination may geminate consonants in the L+. This issue is never discussed in materials aimed at English$_{L+}$ teachers. Whether this is an issue worth addressing will be the teacher's decision, depending on the importance attached to accentedness. Teachers should decide what is the best pronunciation to teach their students in light of both current developments in L+ theorising and what their students want. The present study found that Italian high-school students highly value a native-like pronunciation, and students' desires are an important factor for instructional decisions, albeit not the only one.

Second, in spite of the lack of results of the teaching intervention reported in Chapter 5, teachers may still explicitly teach L+ GPCs (called 'phonics' in English-speaking educational circles), in a way that is suitable for the linguistic and orthographic background of the students. One cannot conclude that training is ineffective just because a one-off half-hour intervention was not successful. In particular, we do not know whether GPC teaching may be effective earlier in the learning process, perhaps at the very beginning when English orthography is introduced. GPCs could be discussed in the context of learners' native phonology and orthography, based on the findings of research on OEs or, if there is no research evidence, using a contrastive approach. Clearly, phonics lessons devised for English native children do not need to state that doublets do not represent long consonants, but this may help English$_{L+}$ learners whose L1 has geminates. Explaining that English doublets do not represent geminates may be useful regardless of whether the L1 uses doublets or other marks for gemination, as doublet-induced gemination was also found in Japanese speakers of English, whose L1 marks gemination with a different symbol. Teachers will need to wait for research to find out whether other types of training can help.

Third, teachers should not expect gemination to be reduced with more exposure to native-speaker input, such as study abroad or native-speaking teachers. Years of naturalistic exposure had limited effects on this study's immigrants to the United Kingdom, possibly because they perceive geminates in English native-speaker input (Chapter 5).

It is too early to draw other conclusions. For instance, researchers proposed to teach words' phonological forms first and introduce word spellings later (Rafat & Perry, 2019), but the proposal has not been tested. Indeed, it is not known whether, once established, a L+ lexical representation is robust enough that it cannot be modified by later exposure to orthographic forms or whether it would be modified reflecting the word's spelling. This is an empirical question that is worth investigating. It is hoped that the rapidly increasing body of empirical evidence will provide answers to this and other issues related to the teaching of L+ phonology.

Envoy

The project reported in this book aimed at providing a blueprint for future research on OEs on L+ phonology. The project made contributions to evidence, theory, and methods, both within and beyond applied linguistics. It is hoped that this project will provide inspiration for researchers and language teachers to further explore this exciting topic.

References

Barrios, S. L., & Hayes-Harb, R. (2020). Second language learning of phonological alternations with and without orthographic input: Evidence from the acquisition of a German-like voicing alternation. *Applied Psycholinguistics, 41*(3), 517–545. https://doi.org/10.1017/S0142716420000077

Bassetti, B. (2008). Orthographic input and second language phonology. In T. Piske & M. Young-Scholten (Eds.), *Input matters in SLA* (pp. 191–206). Multilingual Matters. https://doi.org/10.21832/9781847691118-013

Bassetti, B. (2017). Orthography affects second language speech: Double letters and geminate production in English. *Journal of Experimental Psychology: Learning, Memory, and Cognition, 43*(11), 1835–1842. https://doi.org/10.1037/xlm0000417

Bassetti, B. (2024). Orthographic effects in the phonetics and phonology of second language learners and users. In M. Amengual (Ed.), *The Cambridge Handbook of bilingual phonetics and phonology*. Cambridge University Press.

Bassetti, B., & Cook, V. J. (2011). Language and cognition: The second language user. In V. J. Cook & B. Bassetti (Eds.), *Language and bilingual cognition* (pp. 143–190). Psychology Press.

Bassetti, B., & Filipović, L. (2022). Researching language and cognition in bilinguals. *International Journal of Bilingualism, 26*(1), 3–12.

Bassetti, B., Mairano, P., Masterson, J., & Cerni, T. (2020). Effects of orthographic forms on L2 speech production and phonological awareness, with consideration of speaker-level predictors. *Language Learning, 70*(4), 1218–1256. https://doi.org/10.1111/lang.12423

Bassetti, B., Masterson, J., Cerni, T., & Mairano, P. (2021). Orthographic forms affect speech perception in a second language: Consonant and vowel length in L2 English. *Journal of Experimental Psychology: Human Perception and Performance, 47*(12), 1583–1603. https://doi.org/10.1037/xhp0000949

Bassetti, B., Sokolović-Perović, M., Mairano, P., & Cerni, T. (2018). Orthography-induced length contrasts in the second language phonological systems of L2 speakers of English: Evidence from minimal pairs. *Language and Speech, 61*, 577–597. https://doi.org/10.1177/0023830918780141

Best, C. T., & Tyler, M. D. (2007). Nonnative and second-language speech perception: Commonalities and complementarities. In M. J. Munro & O.-S. Bohn (Eds.), *Language experience in second-language speech learning: In honor of James Emil Flege* (pp. 13–34). John Benjamins.

Browning, S. R. (2004). *Analysis of Italian children's English pronunciation.* Report contributed to the EU FP5 PF STAR Project, led by Martin Russell. Retrieved June 1, 2021, from www.eee.bham.ac.uk/russellm/ItalianEnglishReport/ItalianEnglish_report_v2.htm

Cook, V. J., & Bassetti, B. (2005). An introduction to researching second language writing systems. In V. J. Cook & B. Bassetti (Eds.), *Second language writing systems* (pp. 1–67). Multilingual Matters.

De Clercq, B., Simon, E., & Crocco, C. (2014). Rosa versus rossa: The acquisition of Italian geminates by native speakers of Dutch. *Phrasis: Studies in Language and Literature, 2*(2), 3–29.

Escudero, P., Hayes-Harb, R., & Mitterer, H. (2008). Novel second-language words and asymmetric lexical access. *Journal of Phonetics, 36*(2), 345–360. https://doi.org/10.1016/j.wocn.2007.11.002

Esposito, A., & Di Benedetto, M. G. (1999). Acoustical and perceptual study of gemination in Italian stops. *Journal of the Acoustical Society of America, 106*(4), 2051–2062. https://doi.org/10.1121/1.428056

Flege, J. E., & Bohn, O.-S. (2021). The revised speech learning model (SLM-r). In R. Wayland (Ed.), *Second language speech learning: Theoretical and empirical progress* (pp. 3–83). Cambridge University Press. https://doi.org/10.1017/9781108886901.002

Maddieson, I. (1984). *Patterns of sounds.* Cambridge University Press.

Mairano, P., Bassetti, B., Sokolović-Perović, M., & Cerni, T. (2018a). Effects of L1 orthography and L1 phonology on L2 English pronunciation. *Revue Française de Linguistique Appliquée, 23*(1), 45–57. https://doi.org/10.3917/rfla.231.0045

Mairano, P., Santiago, F., & Delais-Roussarie, E. (2018b). *Gémination non native en français d'apprenants italophones.* In M. Cooke, B. Bigi, & E. Delais-Roussarie (Eds.), *Actes des Journées d'Etudes sur la Parole (JEP 2018)* (pp. 657–665). Aix-en-Provence.

Mitterer, H. (2021). The role of orthography in learning a second language: Evidence from Maltese English. *Xjenza Online, 9*(3), 162–172. https://doi.org/10.7423/XJENZA.2021.3.09

Muneaux, M., & Ziegler, J. C. (2004). Locus of orthographic effects in spoken word recognition: Novel insights from the neighbour generation task. *Language and Cognitive Processes, 19*(5), 641–660. https://doi.org/10.1080/01690960444000052

Nawafleh, A. (2022). L'interférence de la gémination dans la prononciation des étudiants arabophones apprenant le français [The interference of gemination in the pronunciation of Arabic-speaking students learning French]. *Electronic Journal of Foreign Language Teaching [e-FLT]*, *19*(1), 85–98. https://doi.org/https://doi.org/10.56040/anig1916

Piske, T., Flege, J. E., MacKay, I. R. A., & Meador, D. (2002). The production of English vowels by fluent early and late Italian-English bilinguals. *Phonetica*, *59*, 49–71. https://doi.org/10.1159/000056205

Rafat, Y. (2016). Orthography-induced transfer in the production of English-speaking learners of Spanish. *The Language Learning Journal*, *44*(2), 197–213. https://doi.org/10.1080/09571736.2013.784346

Rafat, Y., & Perry, S. J. (2019). Navigating orthographic issues in the teaching of Spanish pronunciation. In R. Rao (Ed.), *Key issues in the teaching of Spanish pronunciation: From description to pedagogy* (pp. 237–253). Routledge.

Rafat, Y., Whitford, V., Joanisse, M. F., Swiderski, N., Cornwell, S., Mohaghegh, M., Valdivia, C., Fakoornia, N., Nasrollahzadeh, P., & Habibi, L. (2021). First-language-specific orthographic effects in second-language speech: A comparison of Korean–English and Farsi–English bilinguals. *Journal of Monolingual and Bilingual Speech*, *3*(1), 102–122. https://doi.org/10.1558/jmbs.15682

Repetti, L. (2009). Gemination in English loans in American varieties of Italian. In A. Calabrese & L. Wetzels (Eds.), *Loan phonology*. John Benjamins.

Sadakata, M., & McQueen, J. M. (2013). High stimulus variability in nonnative speech learning supports formation of abstract categories: Evidence from Japanese geminates. *Journal of the Acoustical Society of America*, *134*(2), 1324–1335. https://doi.org/10.1121/1.4812767

Sokolović-Perović, M., Bassetti, B., & Dillon, S. (2020). English orthographic forms affect L2 English speech production in native users of a non-alphabetic writing system. *Bilingualism: Language and Cognition*, *23*(3), 591–601. https://doi.org/10.1017/s136672891900035x

Sorianello, P. (2014). Italian geminate consonants in L2 acquisition. In L. Costamagna & C. Celata (Eds.), *Consonant gemination in first and second language acquisition* (pp. 25–46). Pacini Editore.

Taft, M. (2006). Orthographically influenced abstract phonological representation: Evidence from non-rhotic speakers. *Journal of Psycholinguistic Research*, *35*, 67–78. https://doi.org/10.1007/s10936-005-9004-5

Young-Scholten, M., & Langer, M. (2015). The role of orthographic input in second language German: Evidence from naturalistic adult learners' production. *Applied Psycholinguistics*, *36*(1), 93–114. https://doi.org/10.1017/s0142716414000447

Zampini, M. L. (1994). The role of native language transfer and task formality in the acquisition of Spanish spirantization. *Hispania*, *77*(3), 470–481. https://doi.org/10.2307/344974

Ziegler, J. C., & Ferrand, L. (1998). Orthography shapes the perception of speech: The consistency effect in auditory word recognition. *Psychonomic Bulletin and Review*, *5*, 683–689. https://doi.org/10.3758/bf03208845

Index

Note: Page numbers in *italics* indicate a figure and page numbers in **bold** indicate a table on the corresponding page.

accentedness: focus 6–7; negative effect of orthography 14
acoustic analysis 41
acoustic cues 30–31
addition 15; sound additions/omissions/substitutions, orthographic forms (impact) 14–18
age of onset of acquisition (AOA), L+ phonology variable 5
age of onset of bilingualism 21
allographs, presence 89
allophones 18
analysis of variance (ANOVA) 42
angle brackets, usage 3
articulation: manner 3; placement 3
articulators, position 3
articulatory features, usage 2–3
auditory and orthographic input (AOI) 49; group 75; impact 12; learner exposure 82; spellings 51; usage 22
auditory-orthographic integration 18
Auditory-Visual Input 71
awareness 92; open questions, usage 40; task, usage 40; training 83

bilabials 3
bilingualism, onset (age) 21
bilinguals: defining 37–38; naturalistic exposure 104–105; orthography, influence (absence) 95–96; recruitment 40
Buizza, Emanuela 29, 41

categorical perception, effects of L1 4
C-CC homophones 71
C-CC homophonic word pairs, usage 67
CC-consonants: duration 84–85; presence 47
CC-C pairs 80
C-CC pairs, sounds (differences) 69
CC:C ratio 51, 53, 54, 57, 59–60; mean CC:C ratio 94–95; reduction 74
C-CC rhyme judgment task, performance (improvement) 74
C-CC rhymes 63, 79; acceptance 82
C-consonants, duration 84–85
C-C pairs 80
CC-pseudowords 79–80
CC-spelling 71
CC-word: orthographic representation 103; semantic activation 73
Cerni, Tania 29, 75
Chinese tones, effects of orthography 13
cognitive individual differences (English$_{L+}$ variable) 58
comprehensibility, focus 6–7
confounds 104–105
Consonant Perception Task 104; Auditory-Visual Input, usage 71

consonants: description, articulatory
features (usage) 2–3;
description, doublet (usage)
89; duration, usage 60; IPA
symbols, usage 3; length
contrast, acoustic cue 30–31;
letters, doublet (correspondence)
32; predictors 60; production,
gemination (presence)
95; production, impact of
orthography 46–55; tokens
31–32; transcription 30
continua, categorisation 100–101
contrastive consonant length, usage 82
Course in General Linguistics
(de Saussure) 10
cross-linguistic influence, effects 4;
see also transfer
C-spelling 71, 76

data cleaning 42
De Iacovo, Valentina 29, 41
Delayed Word Repetition Task,
schematic representation *50*
descriptive statistics, usage 41–42
discontinuous grapheme 15
discrimination, ease 5–6
double consonant letters, impact 33
double letters (doublets): spellings 42,
93, 104; usage 31, 46, 75–82
doublet *see* CC entries; double letters
durational differences: absence 97–98;
perception 66, 67

English consonants 29–30; inventories
30; length 32; singleton/
geminate, Italian$_{L1}$ speaker
categorisation 63–66
English GPCs: Italians' English
orthographic knowledge,
discrepancy 89
English homophonic words, pairs
(usage) 54
English$_{L+}$ consonant perception,
orthographic form (impact) 67,
69, 71

English$_{L+}$ consonants, geminates
(relationship) 82–85
English$_{L+}$ consonants, production/
categorisation reduction 82–85;
design **83**; discussion 85; GPC
instruction *84*; results **85**
English (contrastive consonant length,
absence), learning (impact)
82–85; design **83**; discussion
85; GPC instruction *84*;
results **85**
English$_{L+}$ exposure/use (variable) 58
English$_{L+}$ geminates: perception/
production/categorisation
(correlation) 74; production/
categorisation, elimination/
reduction (absence) 85
English$_{L+}$ gemination: causes 60–61,
94–95; individual-level
predictors 57–59; occurrence
89; predictors 59–60; variables
57–58
English$_{L+}$ (singleton/geminate
consonants), Italian$_{L1}$ listener:
correct answers, mean
percentage *70, 72*; experiment,
design **68, 71**; perception
experiment, schematic *68*;
predictions **69**; predictions/
results **70, 72**
English$_{L+}$ (singleton/geminate
consonants), Italian$_{L1}$ listener
perception 66–72; correct
answers, mean percentage
70, 72; discussion 72–73;
experiment, design **68, 71**;
perception experiment,
schematic *68*; predictions **69**;
predictions/results **70, 72**
English$_{L+}$ (singleton/geminate
consonants), Italian$_{L1}$
speaker categorisation
63–66; experiment, design
64; predictions/results **65**;
qualitative data 64, 66;
results 64; Rhyme Judgment

Index

Task, correct answers (mean percentage) 65
English$_{L+}$ (singleton/geminate consonants), Italian$_{L1}$ speaker production: consonant spelling, impact 46–55; design, summary **47**, **49**, **52**; predictions/results **47**, **51**, **53**; question 46–50; ['sɪtɪ] and ['kɪtɪ], spectrograms *48*
English$_{L+}$ learning (variable) 58
English$_{L+}$ mental lexicons, English$_{L+}$ word representations (presence) 89
English$_{L+}$ orthographic knowledge, GPC rule (inclusion) 89
English$_{L+}$ phonological system, length (feature) 89
English$_{L+}$ word representations, presence 89
English orthographic minimal pairs, production 57
English phonology, mental representations 89
English proficiency self-rating, usage 40
English proficiency test, usage 39–40
English vowel duration 99
English words, production 29
English writing system: allographs (presence) 89; description 7–8
environmental variables, L+ phonology variable 5
environmental written language, exposure 101
epenthetic vowels, addition 15
Escudero, Paola 11
eye-tracking, usage 105

false gemination (syntactic gemination) 30
first (native) language (L1) acquisition 1
first language phonology, effects 4–5
French GPCs, vowel substitutions 17

Geminate consonants: categorisation 91; CC-word categorisation 79–81; CC-word usage 77–79; doublet representation 32; doublet spelling, impact 75–82; durations (production experiments) *52*, 53–54; perception 98; presence 89, 95; representation, consonant doublet (usage) 89
geminate consonants: contrast 28; Italian$_{L1}$ listener perception 66–72; Italian$_{L1}$ speaker production 46–55; singleton consonants, contrast 48, 85–86, 89
geminate consonants, Italian$_{L1}$ speaker categorisation 63–66; experiment, design **64**; predictions/results **65**; Rhyme Judgment Task, correct answers (mean percentage) *65*
geminate:singleton ratios 53–54
gemination: emergence 32; establishment 81; frequency 31–32; levels, elevation 58; lexical contrast 90; presence 101–102; reduction, expectation (absence) 106–107; trigger, double consonant letters (impact) 33
grapheme-phoneme correspondence (GPC) 7–8, 95; discussion 106; doublet understanding 82–83; instruction 83, *84*; Italian GPCs, usage 32; L1-influenced unattested GPCs 19; novel unattested GPCs 19; overgeneralized GPCs 19; rule, inclusion 89; unfamiliar GPCs 19
graphemes: presence 66; representation 17; symbol set 7; pronunciation (determination), GPC (usage) 7
graphotactic rules 19

Hayes-Harb, Rachel 11
heterographic rhymes 64

implications 99–107
incongruent GPCs 22
individual-level predictors 21–22

Index   113

individual variables, L+ phonology variable 5
instructed learners: sequential bilinguals, comparison 55; teaching session, creation 83
integrative motivation, impact 5
intelligibility: focus 6–7; positive effect 14
inter-individual variability 54
International Phonetic Alphabet (IPA), usage 3
intervocalic geminates, production 95
intervocalic position 31
intervocalic voiceless stop consonants, production 53
IoLab response box (perception task) 41
IRIS 40
Italian consonants 29–30; inventories *30*; length 30–32
Italian geminate voiceless stop consonants, median duration *31*
Italian GPCs, usage 32
Italian$_{L1}$-English$_{L+}$ bilinguals (English$_{L+}$ consonant perception), orthographic form (impact) 67, 69, 71
Italian$_{L1}$ gemination, lexical contrast 54–57; design, summary **54**; *finish/Finnish*, spectrograms *56*; predictions/results **56**
Italian$_{L1}$ speakers: singleton/geminate production 46–55
Italian phonological system, singleton/geminate consonants (contrast) 89
Italian geminate and singleton voiceless stop consonants, median duration *31*
Italian writing system, singleton/geminate representation 89
item-level predictors of orthographic effects 22; of gemination 57
items, variables (relationship) 60

L0 learners 13
L1 gemination, variables (relationship) 60
L1-influenced unattested GPCs 19
L1-L+ in-between sounds 18
L1 phonological acquisition, process 97
L1 phonological categories 96
L1 sounds 18, 102
L1 writing system 21
labiodentals, components (involvement) 3
language: exposure, early stages 36; impact 100; plus language 10, 88; processing research, implications 102–103; teaching, implications 106–107
later-learnt language, monolingual/native speaker (qualification) 6
L+ (plus language) 10
L+ awareness: consonant categorisation 63–66; discussion 72–73; findings 85–86; orthography, effects 63
L+ consonant length, contrast 97
learned CC-words: consonants, geminate categorisation 79–81; production, geminate (usage) 77–79
learning, findings 85–86
learning session, example *76*
length mark, IPA symbols (usage) 3
letter-doublet orthographic contrast 88
lexical gemination (true gemination) 30; occurrence, intervocalic position 31
lexical learning 74–82; studies 92
linguistic relativism (relativity) 33–35; continua categorisation (impact) 100–101; language, multi-competent use (relationship) 101; predictions 35
linguistic relativity, written language effects 100
linguistic relativity (evidence), language (impact) 100
L+/L0 phonological learning/processing, facilitation 14
L+ learners, discussion 2
L+ learning 74–86; orthography, effects 63
L+ lexical acquisition (facilitation), orthographic forms (usage) 11–12

loanwords: importation 33; phonology/ L+ phonology, relationship (clarification) 99; word-final position 31
long-short contrast, occurrence 60–61
L+ orthographic input, facilitative effects 11–14
L+ orthographic knowledge 20
L+ orthography 1, 7
L+ perception: development 6; orthography, effects 63
L+ phonological development 91–92
L+ phonology (second language phonology): concepts 1; defining 1–2; development, models 5; learning, goals 6–7; loanword phonology, relationship (clarification) 99; OEs, study 103–104; orthography, negative effects 14–18; perceptions 37; research, issues 3–7; research, object 2–3; variables 5; variables, impact 21
L+ phonology, orthographic effects 10; acoustic analysis 41; case study 28; characteristics/cause/implications 88; confounds, usage 104–105; evidence 32–33; findings **90**; findings, significance 88, 91–92; findings, summary 88–91; future research, limitations/areas 104–106; language processing research implications 102–103; language teaching, implications 106–107; methodological implications 103–104; OE research, confirmation/extension 92–99; OEs, locus 102–103; research questions **90**, 90–91; sample selection 105; tasks/materials, usage 105–106; theoretical implications 101–102
learner events, sequence *39*; linguistic background 29–32; linguistic relativism 33–35; materials, usage 40; methods 37–42; methods, innovation 36; model reduction 42; multi-competence 33–35; participants, characterization **38**; participants, testing 37–40; participation, ethical considerations 41; preliminary data cleaning 42; procedures/equipment 40–41; project, characteristics 35–37; project, history 28–29; publications, usage **34**; rationale 32–33; relativism 33–35; research project 28–35; research questions 32–33, **34**; statistical analysis 41–42; theoretical background 33–35
L+ pronunciation: effect 58; OE research 10
L+ sounds: allophones 18; analysis 104; differences 17; perception/production, L+ orthographic forms (impact) 13–14
L+ speech production 66–73; findings 60–61; focus 6–7; orthography, effects 46
L+ users (sequential bilinguals): language acquisition 2; orthographic knowledge 18–20
L+ words (perception/production), L+ orthographic forms (impact) 13–14
L+ writing systems 7–8, 19–20; learner reliance 21

Mairano, Paolo 29, 41
Masterson, Jackie 29
memory tasks, usage 40
metalinguistic awareness 28
morphemes, concatenation (consequence) 32
morphemic spelling 15
motivation/attitudes (English$_{L+}$ variable) 58
multi-competence 33–35; approach 35
multi-letter grapheme, usage 15

multi-letter morphemic spelling 15
multimodal input, research 12

naïve learners 13
native-like pronunciation, value 106
natives, recruitment 40
naturalistic exposure 59
negative evidence, absence 98
Nodari, Rosalba 29, 41
non-contrastive gemination, presence 98
non-target-like input 97–98
novel unattested GPCs 19
null results 20

omission 16; sound additions/omissions/substitutions, orthographic forms (impact) 14–18
one-to-two scenario 97
Open Science Framework (OSF) 40, 58
orthographic depth 8
orthographic effects (OEs) 6; categorisation, discussion 18; cause 18–20; identification 92; locus 102–103; multiple causes 19; participants, viewpoint (importance) 92; pervasive OE 92; predictors 21–23; study 103–104; usage 77; variability 20, 21–23
orthographic effects (OEs) research 10; confirmation/extension 92–99; experimental results, explanation (qualitative data usage) 37; history 10–11
orthographic forms: impact 14–18; integration 102; usage 11–12
orthographic input: impact, absence 96; presence/absence *12*; effect 49–51; role, clarification 49
orthographic knowledge 18–20
orthographic/phonological representations, co-activation/conflict 102
orthographic representations, impact 13–14
orthography, effects 10, 28, 47, 63, 74

orthography-induced geminates: production 49, 57; usage 66–67
orthography-induced gemination: elimination/reduction, naturalistic exposure (impact) 51; explanation 101–102; Italian production (effect) 49–51; reduction, teaching (impact) 91
orthography-induced omissions, occurrence 16
orthography-induced phonological contrast 36
orthography-influenced L+ phonological representations 103
orthography-influenced phonological representations 102
orthography, learning 103
orthography-phonology correspondence 36
orthography-phonology interface 35–36
orthography-phonology relationship 73–74
outcome sound 94–95
overgeneralized GPCs 19

pairwise comparisons, usage 64
palatalisation, marking 22
palatalised consonants, effects 13
perception experiment, schematic *68*
perception materials spelling task, usage 40
perception-production-awareness connection 73–74
perception task, usage 40
Perceptual Assimilation Model (PAM-L2) 5–6, 101, 102
pervasive OE 92
phonatory system, parts 3
phoneme-grapheme correspondence (PGC) 7–8
phonemes (speech sounds) 2
phonetic distortions 10
phonetic input, basis 6
phonetics, investigation 2
phonological aptitude, impact 5
phonological awareness, effects 4

phonological categories (L1) 96
phonological context 46–47
phonological contrasts 48; difficulty 13; English$_{L1}$ speakers, learning 20; impact 89
phonological learning 74
phonological process 22–23
phonological repertoire, linguistic descriptions 97
phonological representations 102
phonological short-term memory, impact 5
phonological system, phonological categories 88–89
phonological transparency, degrees (differences) 8
phonology, defining 2
phonotactics 3, 19
phrase learning 49; steps 51
plus language 10, 88
power analysis 104
Praat software, usage 41
predicted/observed word-pair ratios **78**
predictors 21–23; individual-level predictors 21–22; item-level predictors 22; task-level predictors 22–23
preliminary data cleaning 42
primary-school children, reading ability 91
primary stress, IPA symbols (usage) 3
pronunciation learning (English$_{L+}$ variable) 58
pseudowords: creation 23; geminate, presence 76; learning 11–12, 81–82; need 36; spoken pseudowords, learning (mean percentage) *12*; usage 13

regression analyses, usage 58
RePsychLing package, rePCA function 42
rhotics, difficulty 13
Rhyme Judgment Task 64, 79; correct answers, mean percentage *65*
roman alphabet, usage 106

romanised Chinese spelling, impact 28
R software, usage 42

secondary stress, IPA symbols (usage) 3
second language (L2) acquisition 1
Second Language Linguistic Perception Modle (L2LP) 6
second language phonology 1
self-perceived proficiency 105
sequential bilinguals, instructed learners (comparison) 55
single-category L1 sounds 102
single consonant letter, usage 89
singleton consonants: contrast 28; durations, production experiments *52*, 53–54; geminate consonants, contrast 51, 85–86, 89; Italian$_{L1}$ speaker production 46–55; presence 89; representation, single consonant letter (usage) 89
singleton consonants, Italian$_{L1}$ listener perception 66–72; correct answers, mean percentage *70*, *72*; discussion 72–73; experiment, design **68**, **71**; perception equipment, schematic *68*; predictions **69**; predictions/results **70**, **72**
singleton consonants, Italian$_{L1}$ speaker categorisation 63–66; experiment design **64**; predictions/results **65**; Rhyme Judgment Task, correct answers (mean percentage) *65*
singleton-geminate contrast, usage 54
['sɪtɪ] and ['kɪtɪ], spectrograms *48*
slashes, usage 3
Sokolović-Perović, Mirjana 29, 41
sound: additions/omissions/substitutions, orthographic forms (impact) 14–18; duration 2; outcome sound 94–95; production, characteristics 2; spelling (determination), PGC (usage) 7; substitutions 94
sound-level variables 59

Southern British English, female native speakers (audio recordings) 40
speech: features 2; production/awareness/spelling, link 82; transcription, International Phonetic Alphabet (IPA) usage 3
Speech Learning Model, revised (SLM-r) 6, 101
speech perception: effects 4; findings 85–86
speech production: effects 4; examination 2
speech sounds (phonemes) 2; segments, division 2
spelling: impact 63–72; pronunciations 10
spoken English: durational differences, perception 67; words (geminate, presence), Italian$_{L1}$ speakers learning (doublet spelling, impact) 75–82; correct answers, predicted/observed mean percentages **80**; design **75**; discussion 81–82; learning session *76*; predicted/observed word-pair ratios **78**; production/awareness *77*; results **79, 81**; spelling tasks *77*, 81; testing session *77*
spoken input, exposure 21–22
spoken language, representation 7
spoken pseudowords, learning (mean percentage) *12*
square brackets, usage 3
Standard British English, consonant systems 29–30, *30*
Standard Italian, consonant systems 29–30; inventories *30*
statistical analysis 41–42
substitution 16–18; sound additions/omissions/substitutions, orthographic forms (impact) 14–18
syllable break, IPA symbols (usage) 3
syllable-final consonant cluster 55
syntactic gemination (false gemination) 30

target consonant 46
target language, phonological repertoire 36
target-like input 97
target-like speech, non-contrastive gemination (presence) 98
target-like spoken input, durational differences (absence) 97–98
target-like spoken percepts, ignoring 97–98
target voiceless stop, word pairs 52
target word production 49; steps 49, 51
target word, replacement 53
task-level predictors 22–23
transfer 101; effects 4; *see also* cross-linguistic influence
transparency level, clarity (absence) 21
triangulation, amount (limitation) 105–106
triphthong, spelling 16
true gemination (lexical gemination) 30
two-category L1 sounds 102
two-to-one category 96

uncategorised L1 sounds 102
unfamiliar GPCs 19

variability 20, 21–23
velar fricative, recoding 20
velar-uvular contrasts 20
voiced alveolar liquid 102
voiced stops, usage 16–17
voiced uvular fricative, usage 102
voiceless alveolar stop 2–3
voiceless stop 46–47
voicing 2–3
vowels: IPA symbols, usage 3; length, determination 17; length, effects 13; pronunciation error correction 14; substitutions 17

word-final position 16, 22, 31, 55
word-final voiced obstruent consonants, substitution 5
word-initial position 16
word-level variables 59

word-pair predictions 78
word-pair ratios, prediction/
    observation **78**
word practice 84
word reading aloud task, usage 40, 47
Word Spelling Task, usage 53, 67

words, variables (relationship) 60
writing systems 7–8
written input, exposure 21–22
written language: environmental written
    language, exposure 101;
    source 100

For Product Safety Concerns and Information please contact our EU
representative GPSR@taylorandfrancis.com
Taylor & Francis Verlag GmbH, Kaufingerstraße 24, 80331 München, Germany

www.ingramcontent.com/pod-product-compliance
Lightning Source LLC
Chambersburg PA
CBHW071512150426
43191CB00009B/1493